"FROM A SPARK TO A FLAME"

THE Chris de Burgh STORY

by

DAVE THOMPSON

Omnibus Press

"FROM A SPARK TO A FLAME"

© Copyright 1987 Omnibus Press
(A Division of Book Sales Limited)

Edited by *Chris Charlesworth*
Art Direction by *Mike Bell*
Book Designed by *Stylorouge*
Picture research by *Chris de Burgh*
Co-ordinated by *Caroline Watson*

Typeset by A J Latham Ltd.

ISBN 0.7119.0976.8
Order No. OP 43892

Exclusive distributors:
Book Sales Limited
8/9 Frith Street, London W1V 5TZ,
UK.

Music Sales Corporation
24 East 22nd Street, New York,
NY 10010, USA.

Omnibus Press
GPO Box 3304, Sydney,
NSW 2001, Australia.

To the Music Trade only:
Music Sales Limited
8/9 Frith Street, London W1V 5TZ,
UK.

Photo credits: The vast majority
of photographs that appear in
this book were contributed by
Chris de Burgh himself, his family,
friends and professional colleagues,
notably Glenn Morrow. The
publishers are grateful for their
use.

A&M Records: 19, 25; Bill Cooper:
35, 44, 65; Paul Cox: 45 (l&b),
GLC: 78 (bl&br); Peter Timm: 49,
76, 84 (1).

Printed by Ebenezer Baylis & Son
Ltd., Worcester.

All lyrics used by permission.

INTRODUCTION

This book is the result of a close
collaboration between myself and the
author, Dave Thompson, and covers
my childhood, my early days in the
music business, and my career to date.
There are many friends I would like
to thank for their help and support
down the years, but I hold a particular
affection for the contributions of
Kenny Thomson, Dave Margereson,
Derek Green, and the boys in the
band. Beyond them are the
thousands, even millions of people all
over the world who have come to my
concerts and enjoyed my music, and
without whom, success and
recognition are just impossible
dreams.
Thank you,

CHRIS DE BURGH

(DEDICATION) For Diane and Rosanna, with all my love

"And when all is said and done
There's only you and me,
You and me"

CHAPTER ONE

WILLIAM FITZADELM DEBURGO, the grandson of William The Conqueror's half brother, arrived in Southern Ireland little less than a century after the Norman conquest of England. Sporadic raiding and uncertain colonisation aside, the land had escaped the fate of her Eastern neighbour until now, but with Norman mercenaries already taking ever larger slices of land for themselves, and the native Kingdoms forever poised on the brink of Civil War, the Norman king Henry II finally decided it was time to take matters in hand.

DeBurgo was of a family whose influence dated back two centuries, whose lineage stretched back even further. Charlemagne, the Frankish founder of the Holy Roman Empire, had held his kinsfolk in high enough esteem to grant one family member the tutelage of 45 towns, or burghs; it was from that honour that the family took its name, midway through the 9th century. Lordships and Earldoms followed; now William DeBurgo was to bring Tipperary under Norman rule. He was created governor of Wexford, and by 1175 was already so powerful that, almost singlehandedly, he was responsible for the Bishops' Synod in that town at which was published Pope Alexander IV's proclamation of Henry II's right to style himself Lord of all Ireland.

Vast estates in both Tipperary and neighbouring Connacht passed to DeBurgo, and in condoning sporadic raiding and ravaging by his Scottish mercenaries, or *galloglaigh*, most of which was intended to replace Cathal Crodberg, King of the O'Conors, with the pretender Cathal Carrack, he effortlessly found his way into contemporary Irish annals as their own William The Conqueror.

There was no church from the Shannon westwards to the sea that they did not pillage or destroy, and they used to strip the priests in the churches and carry off the women without regard to saint or sanctuary or to any power on earth.

(The annals of Loch Ce)

By the time of his death, in 1206, DeBurgo had acquired more land in Ireland than any other Norman family — one reason why DeBurgh, and its variants, Burke and Bourke, even today are recognised as amongst the most numerous of all Hiberno-Norman surnames.

William's son, Richard, succeeded him as governor of Wexford, and in 1215 King John granted him all the lands in Connacht... on the exact same day as he made a similar grant to Cathal Crodberg.

Richard's claim to the area was the weaker of the two; John regarded his charter as little more than a speculative reserve, something to be empowered only in the event of Crodberg's death leading to a power struggle as bitter as that which had marked his succession. This, in 1224, is what happened, and Richard found himself granted unconditional control over the area by King Henry III. He immediately pressed his claim, not only on Connacht, but neighbouring Athlone as well, and that same year saw a massive Norman army defeat the King of Athlone, Aodh, at the Battle of Athlone. The city fell and Norman domination was assured.

It was Richard DeBurgo who built the castles at Galway and Loughrea; very likely it was he, too, who caused to be erected what is now Bargy Castle, in the village of Tomhaggard, the family seat of the DeBurghs since Chris' grandfather purchased it from the Harvey family in November 1960.

In 1296, Richard's son, also named Richard, led more than 1,600 soldiers on the Balliol campaigns against the Scots; eight years later, it was he who received the submission of the Scottish governor, Red John Comyn. However, when Edward Bruce invaded Ireland in 1315, proclaiming himself King of a Celtic Union, Richard was imprisoned by the mayor of Dublin and a deputation sent to the court of King Edward II to decide his fate; Richard's daughter, Elizabeth, was now the wife of Robert The Bruce, Edward Bruce's brother. And despite Richard, as second Earl of Ulster, having long before sworn allegiance to the Crown, suspicions still lingered as to his true sympathies in the imminent conflict.

Richard was released after only a short time, but it was left to his kinsman, the Custos of Ireland, Edmund Bourke, to set the stage for the deaths of both Bruce and the Scottish dream; in 1316, two years before the final battle at Faughart, Edmund routed Bruce's armies at the Battle of Athenry and freed Connacht, at least, from the grip of the invaders.

It was not only Ireland wherein the

DeBurghs made their presence felt in these islands. Hubert DeBurgh, the Earl of Kent and (in most genealogies) brother of William Fitzadelm DeBurgo, was one of King John's chief advisors, and one whom John — according to Shakespeare at least — held in the greatest esteem:

...O My gentle Hubert
We owe thee much! Within this wall of flesh
There is a soul counts thee her creditor
And with advantage means to pay thy love
And, my good friend, thy voluntary oath
Lives in this bosom, deeply cherished

It was Hubert, again according to Shakespeare, who refused John's command to put out the eyes of the infant Prince Arthur of Brittany with red hot coals:

I will not touch thine eye
For all the treasure that thine Uncle owns

Later, towards the end of John's reign, he commanded the port of Dover and repulsed a French invasion. Two years later, in August 1217, it was DeBurgh who led the Cinqe Ports fleet which so effectively demolished another French force, an immense fleet which was bringing armed reinforcements to the French Dauphin, then on a supposed diplomatic mission which only scarcely disguised his claim to the throne of England. The English, windward of their foe, threw quicklime into the faces of the French, then moved in for the kill with swords. The French fled in disarray, limping home in the knowledge that such an ignominious — and unexpected — defeat all but ended Louis' claim; it certainly undermined the Baronial support he had been relying on in his attempt to depose John's infant son, Henry III, as the English ruler.

Because Henry was so young (he was just nine when King John died), Pope Honorius placed the Earl of Pembroke in control of the kingdom; when he passed away in 1219, a second Papal legate was established, with Hubert DeBurgh the justiciar, or chief administrative officer.

His government was vigorous. DeBurgh was a prodigious builder; years before King Edward I finally secured the Welsh Marches with a string of castles, DeBurgh was planning and building his own. One of the finest is at Monmouth where, in 1223, Hubert took the young King Henry to see a site which was,

according to contemporary historian Matthew Parys, "suitable for the erection of an impregnable castle." When completed, the castle had cost the Crown £2,000, and Hubert was granted the right to live there, with an annual stipend of £130 for upkeep.

From Monmouth, Hubert was able to suppress an uprising by the Welsh prince Llewellyn, while elsewhere, the troublesome Barons of King John's day, who had grown increasingly ungovernable even after their support for the Dauphin had proved misplaced, were expelled. But when Henry III finally came of age, in 1227, DeBurgh discovered that his success had by no means made him popular amongst the King's friends. Within five years, Henry had reopened the war with France, despite DeBurgh's advice to the contrary, and filled any vacant offices with foreign advisors. Finally, in 1232, DeBurgh was arrested, charged with "connivance", and deprived of both his offices and his lands. He might even have ended his days in chains, had not Henry been unable to find a smith willing to forge fetters for the man who had so dramatically saved England from the French a decade and a half previous.

Just as England was never again to know such a great justiciar (the office was eventually abandoned), so the DeBurghs were to leave no further such indelible marks on history. They remained in positions of prominence, however.

In Palestine, Godfrey de Bouillon, the irascible uncrowned King of Jerusalem and Advocate of the Holy Sepulchre, dominated the politics of the First Crusade, both personally and, after his death, through his family. Uncle, by marriage, to the English King Stephen, and thus a kinsman of the DeBurgos (a more direct link exists in family mythology and, perhaps, in their pre-Conquest lineage) Godfrey was responsible for establishing a dynasty which endured in the Holy Land for close to 100 years. When his line finally ended, so did Western supremacy over the near-East.

As Holy as Jerusalem was to the Crusaders, it was equally Holy to the forces of Islam; Mohammed had ascended to Heaven from beneath a rock little more than a stone's throw from Golgotha. Second only to Mecca, Jerusalem was sacred to Islam; even without the intervention of the Crusaders, the scene would have been set for a theological battle of immense proportions. With them, it was plunged into a bloodbath as violent as it was ultimately needless. The scenario which Chris paints in 'Crusader', the title track to his fourth album, may not be historically accurate (King Richard the Lionheart was never to see the city of Jerusalem, at least not until Cecil B. DeMille set the struggle down on celluloid), but the mood of the times he captures with slide rule precision. For the humble soldiers, the Crusades were, indeed, an act of faith. To their leaders, however, divided as they were in the power struggles which resulted from the absence of a true ruler, they became a political football, to be kicked about right up until the hoardes of Islam called time and swatted them aside.

●　　　●　　　●

In 1342, Lady Elizabeth DeBurgh, the only child of William, the third Great Earl of Ulster, married Lionel, the Duke of Clarence, the third son of the English King Edward III. Elizabeth was just ten years old at the time of the marriage — which took place in Westminster Abbey — and Lionel was three.

It is from this marriage that the great House of Tudor developed; at the time, however, the marriage was purely political. Through the marriages of his children, Edward III was simply collecting Earldoms. Lionel's inheritance of the Ulster Earldom following the murder of his father-in-law in 1333, was particularly beneficial to Edward's plans. During a lull in his wars with France, the King despatched Lionel to Ireland with a small army to inspect his inheritance and to try and ease the growing tensions between the Irish and their supposed masters. Swiftly perceiving that his military force was by no means sufficient to deal with the problems, Lionel presided over a Parliament at Kilkenny, in 1366, at which an amicable solution to the constant warring

between English colonialists and Irish nationalists was sought. The result was the statute of Kilkenny and the establishment of the English Pale. Within the district bearing this name, centred around Dublin, English law was to be strictly enforced; outside, the Irish chiefs could continue doing exactly as they pleased. The statute forbade Englishmen to marry the Irish, or to adopt Irish customs.

The Statute worked within the English Pale, but without, perpetual disorder prevailed. Finally, in October, 1394, King Richard II paid a personal visit to the country. Appointing his cousin (Lionel and Elizabeth's grandson) Roger de Mortimer governor of Ireland, Richard landed with a massive army and fleet, and campaigned into Leinster, where he defeated King Art MacMurrough. For the other Irish leaders, that was enough. They submitted to English rule, Richard repaying them by granting certain chieftains legal status

and, in a handful of cases, Knighthoods. The recipients of this particular honour, Art MacMurrough included, had put aside their Irish dress and adopted English customs, a sacrifice which Richard regarded as a sign of true loyalty. However, the moment the King's back was turned, his accomplishments collapsed. His policies of reconciliation proved very unpopular with the English colonists, who hated the idea of the Irish being on a level footing with them, and in 1399, Richard was forced to return to Ireland. Landing at Waterford, he marched to Dublin, where he intended settling the colonists' grievances once and for all. However, he was instead greeted with news of Henry Bolingbrooke's insurrection in England and, placing the Irish problem in abeyance, he returned home — to lose both his throne and his head.

The assassination of the Lady Elizabeth DeBurgh's father did much to bring about an

end to the power of the DeBurghs in Ireland. The Ulster Earldom having passed to the Duke of Clarence, and thence to his offspring (the current Earl is the eldest son of the Duke and Duchess of Kent), the DeBurghs changed their name to one which would, within a few generations, blend in with those of their adopted countrymen, Burke and Bourke, and in the case of the ruling caste, MacWilliam.

Not until the 17th Century was this corruption of the family name arrested. One Richard Bourke altered his surname to Burgh upon entering the Anglican ministry in the 1630s, a century later, the 11th Earl of Clanricade, a family line which began in the 1400s and only died out in 1916, re-established his right to assume 'The Ancient Surname' by sign manual. Chris' great-great-grandfather, Thomas, followed suit on March 6, 1848.

General Sir Eric de Burgh, Chris' grandfather.

Henry returned to Ireland in 1846, Robert, the oldest surviving brother of Chris' great-great-grandfather, stayed.

Then there was General Sir Eric DeBurgh, Chris' maternal grandfather, whose career began in the Boer War in South Africa at the turn of the century, took him through the First World War and Waziristan, and finally deposited him in India during the final two decades of British colonial rule. Between 1939 and 1941, he was Chief of General Staff in India and, remembers Chris, "He told marvellous stories about the Khyber Pass and the Northern Front. He once trekked alone across the Pass to talk with warring tribesmen who were pinning down thousands of British troops, who were needed to fight in Europe. He went over, and he met an ancient old tribal leader, and they struck a bargain; there would be no more fighting on that frontier for ten years, and the British troops would be set free to fight in Europe. I think the tribesman was impressed with the courage of this man who came alone through hostile territory to meet him." Upon his death, the General was buried, as was his wish, in the gold and wool kaftan presented to him by the frontier chief as a token of respect.

"My grandfather had many stories about elephant parades. He was in charge of 100 elephants the day that someone tried to murder the Viceroy by throwing a bomb at him. The elephants all stampeded, and it was my grandfather who brought them all back under control."

Another story which made a terrific impact on Chris, and which he drew on for a song on his second album, 'This Song For You', concerned the future General's time in France during the Great War. "Both my grandfather and his brothers fought out there; one, Thomas DeBurgh, was the first Allied soldier to be killed in the War (on September 14th, 1914). His father, my great-grandfather, was too old to serve, so instead he bought an ambulance and drove across to Flanders. There's a story about how my grandfather, having spent the entire night up to his waist in mud, was walking behind the lines towards a crossroads. Stumbling through the rain and mud, he saw an ambulance, and out of it stepped his father! They embraced, and his father gave him a bottle of brandy. He said it saved his life that day. They didn't meet up again until after the war."

The General retired from service in 1941. In that year he was awarded the KCB, his third military honour (in 1916 he won a DSO, eight years later an OBE). A decade on, his eldest daughter, Maeve Emily, returned home from Argentina with Charles Davison, her husband of five years, and their two children, Richard Charles and his younger brother Christopher John.

Members of Parliament and high-ranking clergy (Ulysses Burgh was rewarded for his support of William of Orange against James II with the Bishopric of Ardagh; four generations later, Thomas John DeBurgh was Dean of Cloyne), all played their part not only in the history of the DeBurgh family, but in the history of Ireland itself. Ulich Negan, the first Earl of Clanricade was feared throughout 16th Century Ulster; Negan means The Beheader, and Ulich liked nothing better than to tour battlefields, beheading the corpses and stacking the skulls up in great piles. His son, Richard, on the other hand, reflects something of the times in which he lived when we learn he divorced his first wife, Margaret, on the grounds that she had bewitched him!

Other members of the family took the name further afield. Theobald Bourke fled to Spain in 1595 and was created Marquis of MacVilliam Burk by King Philip II, Raymond Bourke was a peer in post-revolutionary France and fought as a commander in Napoleon Bonaparte's army, Statesman Edmund Burke, genealogist John Burke, all play their part in the family tree; so does Robert O'Hara Burke, the first white man to cross Australia from north to south. Another Australian explorer, also named Robert, erected a homestead in Perth which still stands today, a protected building claimed to be one of the oldest continually habited colonial buildings in all of West Australia. It was built in 1850, nine years after Robert, and his brother, Henry, struggled onto dry land, survivors of the wrecked brig, *James Matthews*.

CHAPTER TWO

CHRISTOPHER JOHN DAVISON was born on October 15 1948, on his father's family farm in Argentina, some 200 miles west of the capital, Buenos Aires. The Davisons had been in Argentina since the 1850's, arriving just as the country's economy was making the transition from slavery to free labour. That, coupled with the entire Latin continent's fast growing independence from the Spanish empire (Argentina was the first to break free, in 1810), made this particular corner of the New World seem especially attractive to workers displaced by the Industrial Revolution then spreading throughout Europe.

Between 1857 and 1913, some four and a half million immigrants arrived in Argentina: British, Irish, Spanish, Italian and, in the case of the Davisons, Australian too. Chris told Niall Stokes, of *Hot Press* magazine, "In the area which reputedly has a lot of the best land in Argentina, there were a lot of Welsh, Irish, Scottish and English speaking people. I was, in fact, eligible for conscription into the military services in Argentina because I was born there.

Quite a lot of the young lads who fought in the Falklands on the Argentinian side were in fact of basically British descent, which made the whole thing even worse."

Chris' father's family is of British origin. "They were amongst the first people to go out to Australia as settlers rather than convicts. They are interesting people because a lot of them were engineers on a global scale," Chris remembers. "His grandfather built the Vladivostock railway in Russia. They were all very inventive, very creative people. Another branch of his family were missionaries in Brazil, Africa."

Charles Davison, Chris' father, was born on the island of Jersey in 1915, moving out to the Argentinian farm sometime after the Great War. The farm was being run, in his family's absence, by another family, to whom the Davisons had rented the land; indeed the tenants seem to have so enjoyed their occupancy that the Davisons experienced some difficulty in persuading them to move out once their lease had expired! Thus, they spent some time touring the world before finally returning home, living for short periods in Australia and Spain.

It was to Spain, to Barcelona, that Charles Davison returned in the mid-1930s. He taught

Charles Davison with his son Chris, aged three weeks.

English there until the outbreak of the Spanish Civil War forced him to move back to Argentina; three years later, he was back in Europe, a Royal Navy volunteer at the outbreak of World War Two. Later in the conflict, he moved into the Special Operations Executive and spent four years behind Japanese lines in Burma, organising resistance and sabotage, during which time he made two treks of a thousand miles through the jungle, supported only by his own wits, trying to evade the occupying Japanese armies. Lieutenant Colonel Davison was later awarded the MBE for his work in the Far East.

"I am very proud of what my father did during the War," Chris says. "The more I read and learn about the Japanese war, the more I realise just how horrific it must have been for him. Even today, he refuses to have anything to do with Japanese goods — we bought him a Seiko watch for Christmas one year, and he just couldn't wear it. I laughed at the time, but since then I've come across people who feel the same way about the Germans, and you have to respect their attitude because you simply cannot know what they went through at the time."

Chris was 11 years old when he first set eyes on Bargy Castle, the imposing monument to Ireland's wartorn past which was to figure so heavily in his later life. He fell in love with it immediately, and remembers how, on his first day there, he and his brother Richard discovered a secret passage... "Full of bones and weird kinds of artifacts. There were four sticks of gelignite which had been left there years before, the Army had to come and blow

Above: Chris with his brother Richard, in Nigeria in 1955; and wearing traditional Argentinian dress in 1950.

them up, which left a huge hole in the ground."

Only a small area of the castle was immediately habitable. Although there was upwards of 40 rooms, most of them either hadn't been occupied for years, or had birds living in them — turkeys and pheasants, left by the previous owner. And there was no water. The family had to pump for half an hour every day to get fresh water. It was going to be a pretty hard kind of existence, Chris remembers thinking, but the castle was going to make a great playground as well.

Bargy Castle was to become the first permanent home Chris ever knew. After four years in Argentina, where he began his schooling, the family moved "very briefly", to Ireland, staying with the General at his home in Naas, an idyllic country cottage straight out of the picture books. He had an old, turn of the century house in Naas, county Kildare (the constituency represented two hundred years previous by his forebears). Says Chris, "It was the kind of a place where I'd like my children to grow up, with beautiful lawns, vegetable gardens, the perfect home."

From there, they headed to Malta.

Chris' father was still attached to the SOE; now he was training agents in small arms and weapons, jungle warfare and so on. He tells how Chris threw his first hand grenade, and fired his first sten gun on the underground firing range at Fort Benjemma before his seventh birthday, although Chris himself doesn't remember too much about it.

It was from Fort Benjemma that Charles Davison was involved in the training of agents for espionage behind the Iron Curtain, in Albania. The exiled King Zog's own, battle hardened Royal Guard, together with nearly 300 other exiles and sympathisers, were being sent by the West into Albania, either by parachute or submarine, but their every landfall ended in disaster, Russian troops would be waiting on the exact spot, ready for them. Not one agent returned alive, and yet it was not for three years that the operation was finally halted — and the cause of so many deaths, the British MI6's own Head of Espionage, Kim Philby, became known. Chris admits he gave very little thought to his father's career. "I don't think I knew that much about it at the time, although I'm very interested nowadays. And it quickly becomes obvious that spying is not the romantic thing which it is portrayed as, it is very destructive, even though the real dangers which are involved don't become apparent for a long time after. It's almost as if these things are happening on the very edge of your consciousness; the alarm bells are ringing, but you don't hear them because you're asleep, or because it's windy outside. And then one day, you find out just how critical such and such an event could have been."

Bargy Castle

On leaving the S.O.E., Chris' father moved his family on to Nigeria, where he began work with an earth-moving firm. They remained there for three years, then, at the end of the decade, moved to the Belgian Congo. It was to be a shortlived stay. In 1960, the occupying power pulled out suddenly and unexpectedly. The country was thrown into chaos; whereas the end of British and French rule in the west and east had seen relatively little bloodshed, at that point in time at least, the sprawling Congo erupted, with Europeans the main targets. From the mineral rich province of Katanga, and the high powered attempts to bring separate independence to the one jewel in the Congo's crown at the expense of the rest of the country, Chris' parents fled to the still calm Rhodesia, miles away, Chris' father leading a convoy of around 20 vehicles to safety, through the jungle.

When Chris was seven and a half, and his brother, Richard, was nine, they were both sent away to a boarding school back home in Ireland; Aravan, in Bray. "I was really too young," he believes today, adding, "I could only have been two foot high at the time. Unfortunately, there was simply no alternative way to get a decent education." The boys' parents stayed in Africa, and they only saw them for a few weeks every year. "The thing I remember best about Africa was the marketplaces, the fantastic colours of the dresses the women were wearing, the colours of the beans which were sold, the amazing colour and the bustle. And the friendliness..."

One night, Chris' mother was bitten on the leg by a snake. The ensuing dash to a hospital, nobody knowing for certain whether or not the reptile was poisonous (fortunately, it wasn't), has remained with Chris ever since; while his mother was being examined within, Chris and Richard sat outside in the car, weeping, and fearing the worst. "I was the only member of my family not to be bitten by a snake while we were out there, but I was still pretty scared of them. I still dislike snakes intensely! My brother and I used to go into the bush quite often and look at the wild animals lurking around. But we didn't spend that much time out there, because of the difficulties in getting there during school holidays, and I think being separated from my parents like that had a pretty strong impact on me. I don't think I'm as emotionally upset as I could have been, but it was a little difficult. I think if you can handle it it gives you a very strong feeling of independence. My brother would have preferred less of it, though. Being the first born, he missed his parents a bit more than I did. I had him to lean on because he was my big brother, but he had nobody, so it must have hurt quite a lot.

"I think if I had been badly affected by it, I should have come out as a person who was unable to show affection, but I'm the absolute opposite, I'm a very affectionate person."

During the school holidays the boys would be farmed out to those grim beings who make their living from taking in boys in their kind of position. Rarely did they return to the same family twice. Holidays, then, were something almost to be dreaded: with no

Chris, aged six, in Nigeria

opportunity to even begin building a relationship with their hosts, Chris and Richard did their best to keep themselves to themselves. It was, says Chris, all pretty dismal. "Of course, it was unpleasant for our mother and father too, because they couldn't afford to fly us out to Africa all the time. The best holidays, apart from those when we got to see our parents, were those which we spent with my grandfather, whom I loved dearly."

As close in age as they were (Chris was just 18 months younger than Richard), a certain amount of rivalry was sure to develop between the two brothers, although Chris says he never realised the extent of it until "one day I realised we were doing things which were the total opposite. He loved classical music, I would want to bawl out pop. He played organ, I played piano. He went on to become a lawyer, I went on to do this. I was very much under his shelter when we were younger, but as time went by, so I came out more and more... I became a real show-off, like I was always the one who would get the girls in the pub at night. It wasn't rivalry in the way that we would always be fighting, because we weren't. But brotherly affection is pretty rare, and we did have our ups and downs... nowadays we are much closer!"

Chris remained at the boarding school until he was 12, when he was accepted into the prestigious Marlborough College in Wiltshire, England. His grandfather was an Old Boy, and Chris' name had been on the school's books for several years. Not only was the College rated amongst the top half dozen public schools in Britain, it also had one of the country's highest University acceptance rates.

"I'm one of those people who is basically lazy, but when it comes to the crunch I can work really hard," says Chris of his career at Marlborough. "I am a retentive learner, but I don't like to fill my head with facts months before exams. So I jam it all in at the last moment and get through that way. Marlborough I enjoyed, actually. I loved sports — I was quite good at second level rugby, cricket, soccer... I was a bit of a loner, but not so much that I didn't enjoy those sports, although I must admit, I'd be more likely to play wing half, or centre, rather than get in the middle of the scrum — I don't think I'd have been big enough to be in the scrum! And finally, of course, I'd go home for holidays with these stories about endless parties in London. It must have seemed very glamorous.

"I was very lucky that because of my upbringing and where we lived, I developed an outsider's view of the English. No comparison intended, but one of the nicest things that has happened to the Irish is that they've produced the greatest literary figures of our time. Bernard Shaw, Oscar Wilde, James Joyce, Samuel Beckett... And they all have one thing in common; they went out of Ireland, looked, went back, looked again. And you can get a great overview from that. I really enjoy having that ability, I appreciate it a lot."

It was whilst at Marlborough that Chris first became interested in music. But then, as he says himself, who didn't? It was 1963, and just as seven years earlier, the sight and sound of Elvis Presley on the *Ed Sullivan Show* had finally given American youth something to aim at, living proof that life needn't be spent doing the same things as your parents and your parents' parents, so The Beatles came along to give the youth of Britain a similar jolt.

Before then, British pop music had been lamentable indeed, an endless succession of pasty faced youths launched to five minute superstardom on the back of a pleasant smile and a Tin Pan Alley tunesmith, or guitar groups with glassy grins, all bearing the scars of having watched too many Shadows' routines. Suddenly someone pointed out that it wasn't a chance encounter with a randy entrepreneur in some seedy Soho coffee bar that launched one to stardom, nor was it an ability to ape the biggest hits of the day, never straying from parameters tried and tested so many times in the past. You could make it on your own talents, on your own terms and — this was the big one — with your own songs! Before The Beatles it was unheard of for pop singers to write their own material; even Cliff Richard, positively the most important talent to emerge from the wasteland which was Britain's attempt to leap aboard the rock 'n' roll bandwagon, turned to outside composers for his material. But within 12 months of 'Please Please Me' giving The Beatles their first chart topper, it was unheard of for them not to.

By contemporary standards, Chris was something of a late starter. He was impressed by The Beatles, of course, but it was some years before the realisation hit him that *this is what I want to do.* "I remember going into one of those little booths in a record shop to hear 'Love Me Do', but the first time I became really interested in pop music was when I heard The Byrds' version of 'Mr Tambourine Man', the Bob Dylan song. The intro, with the bass line underneath it, was so extraordinary, it hit me right between the eyes. It was the first time I ever reacted emotionally to a piece of music, apart from church music which I still love.

"Every one at the school had guitars, although to be quite honest about it, the main reason for playing guitar was to attract the fair sex. If you could sit at a party and strum three chords... that's why I learned the guitar! My first guitar came from my brother — I stole it from him. And originally the idea was just to impress the girls — play your cards right and you might get kissed before the night was out. That was the advantage of playing, you'd be sitting in a corner, 'How many roads must a

The interior of Bargy Castle.

man walk down…', all that, and everybody's drunk, nobody's listening, and there's maybe one girl in the corner who's sitting there thinking 'Ah, he's wonderful…'"

Once he learned to play, Chris quickly discovered another outlet for his new found talent. Every summer his parents opened up the castle as a family holiday hotel. It took a lot of work: when they first moved in there was only one bathroom in the entire place. They installed another 21, cutting through the six foot thick stone walls which at times must have seemed as impervious to their efforts as they would have to anyone attempting to break into the castle during its days as a fortress.

"We could take up to 50 people, and for five or six months a year we'd have people staying with us. My brother and I and the whole family would pitch in — I was the wine waiter, I used to spill the soup a lot as well. But it really was like a family gathering. Those were the days when people used to go on family holidays for two or three weeks at a stretch. And I made so many friends, that to this day I still see… really unusual people. All these families used to arrange to meet up together each year at the castle. It really was a fabulous way of growing up."

Every night, Chris would entertain the families with his guitar. "And every teenage girl in the place would be fair game.

"I must have had a repertoire of 400, 500 songs at this time, a lot of covers and a few which I wrote — crappy things… you know you have to write fifty, a hundred, bad songs before you ever come up with a good one. But it was great experience for me. There would be different people there every night and every night I'd subject them to this. Before I ever stood on a concert stage I must have done hundreds and hundreds of these living room performances, and most people simply don't ever get that kind of experience. They can go to a folk club, I suppose, but this was so different to that. There was a very real sense of togetherness. Someone would just say 'Get out your guitar, Chris,' and I'd play."

He also formed a group with a few

friends, Gary Roberts and Simon Crowe (who later found fame with the Boomtown Rats), and Michael Odlum. "It was never a full-time thing, I think the only real thing we did was a dance in Waterford and a few hunt balls. But it was a lot of fun, we shared a lot of very silly experiences, we used to stay up till dawn, raid the wine cellar, and get hopelessly drunk."

It wasn't all excitement, though, as Chris remembers. "In the winter time this bloody castle would get awfully cold. We used to have to go up to bed with all our clothes on. People sometimes look at my upbringing and say it was very privileged, but it was only privileged because my mother and father wanted to create that kind of environment for my brother and myself. We had a farm there, about 200 acres, cattle, sheep, corn, but it was the family who worked on it. And that's been good for me as well, I find myself very much a lover of the land. In the summer you had all these unusual people coming to stay at the hotel, but the rest of the time I was very much a land person, I just loved being in the country.

"The fact is that having a fairly cosmopolitan upbringing gives you a slightly different outlook on things. A lot of British music comes out of the unemployed factor and also the bourgeoisie area, the struggling to become somebody. But I didn't particularly want to be more equal among equals. Right from the start I felt that I was pushing out in my little boat from the shore and setting off in a completely different area. I've never felt that I've joined the mainstream, and I think that every time that I've tried to go a little into the mainstream it's kind of rebounded on me. If you make too strong an attempt to be commercial in music it always leaves a bit of a sour taste, and those people who believed in you right from the start, they sense what you're up to. So, every time I write a song or record an album today, it has to be about something I absolutely stand behind and believe."

Above: Watching for Haley's Comet from the tower of Bargy Castle, December, 1985.
Entertaining guests, including Russell Harty, at Bargy Castle.

Chris left Marlborough College in 1966, having already applied for places at Oxford, Cambridge and Trinity College, Dublin. All three accepted him and for a short time Chris was undecided as to which to enter. Ultimately, the final decision was taken out of his hands. Oxford and Cambridge both required applicants to sit what is known as the Oxbridge exam in September. Chris simply didn't want to wait that long.

He was still not certain how he wanted to spend the rest of his working life, however. Everybody told him that he'd be better off going to Trinity instead of hanging about all summer waiting for the Oxbridge test, and in the end, that was what he did. He spent four years at Trinity, living in a succession of little bedsits around the city centre. "I started off studying Spanish, which I didn't really get into, so I switched and wound up getting a degree in French and English, and a general degree which involved three subjects. Mine were English, French and History."

He was still not certain how he wanted to spend the rest of his working life, however. Music was a very real possibility; as he says, "As a child I had no ambitions. My family tradition has always been individualist, so I suspected that it wouldn't be along a 'traditionalist' route. And my parents were

Main Pic: Chris with Paul Tullio.

very supportive — they knew from my performances in the castle that I was capable of doing it, and that I wasn't the sort of person who would just sit around at home whining all the time, so they never tried to push me into anything else."

Chris swiftly adapted to University life. Paul Tullio, one of his closest friends then and now, and like Chris, a former English Public Schoolboy, remembers: "He always seemed a very quiet chap, he wasn't rowdy or noisy, but he was immense fun to be around. I first met him at Trinity Players (the theatrical side of the University), which is where I used to spend a large amount of my time — as he did. We also wrote for the *TCD Miscellany*, which was the Trinity magazine, together, with Chris contributing the rudest, most vulgar articles under the by-line Dennis Oddfinger. Very silly, very smutty, undergraduate drivel, which is what most people seemed to be into…"

The pair regularly appeared in University revues together, Chris specialising in parodies and comedy roles — and the sillier the better. Says Paul, "Chris has always had a wacky sense of humour like me and he hasn't lost that. He has always been great for telling dirty jokes, and somehow, he has managed to surround himself with people who bring out the worst of it in him… like me. Yet he still writes these lovely little songs, full of romance and beauty."

Aside from his guitar, Chris' pride and joy at the time was his van, a battered old Renault 4 with a sofa in the back. From all accounts, it was a horrible thing; at some point in its life, a couple of pints of milk must have been spilt down the back of it and the smell never left. Nevertheless, Chris and his friends made grateful use of the vehicle, piling down to Bargy Castle in it, with Chris determined never to exceed 25 or 30 mph. Paul still doesn't know if he was just a cautious driver or if he was afraid the van would fall to bits, but remembers the trip used to take close to four hours. Normally, it could have been done in little more than two!

Very early on, Chris became a centre of attraction for a fairly large group of people — including, on one occasion, the local police. One of Chris' favourite games was to organise a stage fight in pubs, himself and a friend apparently beating the living daylights out of each other. On one particular evening, Paul Tullio was called in as Chris' opponent. He remembers, "We started fighting in the bar, took it through the room, rolled out of the door, across the pavement and into the middle of the road. And there we were, when this motorcycle cop pulled up beside us, and went to great pains trying to separate us. He wasn't at all pleased when he discovered it was all a joke, with these two undergraduates grinning foolishly at him."

According to Susan Colgan, another of the Trinity Players, "Chris was always very happy. While everybody else was going through these great angst crises, Chris would be happily wandering around, laughing about everything. You'd be in the middle of relating some awful personal saga to him, and suddenly you'd realise there was just no point in going on with it, because he would always see the funny side of it. It was useless trying to cry on his shoulder, because he simply refused to take anything seriously."

Chris was not without his thoughtful side, though, as he proved when two friends got married. "He gave them a stone," says Susan. "But it wasn't any old stone. It was a beautiful stone, one which he had picked out from the beach at Wexford with great tenderness. He wrapped it up very neatly, and the people he gave it to, I think, were so stunned by it that they actually kept it!"

It was Chris' musical abilities, however, which won him the most acclaim. A Trinity tradition was to take a revue for a late night run at the Wexford Opera festival, every September. 1970 saw Chris, together with James Morris, Julian Salmon and Richard Fegan, take their turn, renting a house just a stone's throw from Bargy Castle as a base of operations. Their engagement was to last ten days, the revue onstage from 11 till midnight every night, and to celebrate, the foursome formed a band — The Jim Flesh Five. Every night, for two and a half hours before going onstage, this inaptly named four-piece would run through their paces in the bar.

James Morris admits, quite happily, that Chris was the musical force in the band. "The rest of us just knew the moves." They played 12-bar blues and Beatles' songs. "The first time I met Chris," says James, "he had his guitar with him. He was the only person I ever knew who had all The Beatles songs off, note-perfect."

Paul Tullio adds, "At parties, people would ask him to bring his guitar along, but after the first half hour, they'd be begging him to put it away again. He was terrific on Beatles' songs, but he would insist on throwing his own ones in as well, and if somebody didn't say something, he'd be quite happy to go on with them all night." And while Paul confesses, "We were all terribly surprised by the standard of some of the songs he wrote, Chris' own songs were usually referred to, not too kindly, as 'Makey-Uppy stuff'.

Even so, he was to enjoy several very real, very genuine triumphs. One year, midway through Chris' life at Trinity, the head of Trinity Players, Mike Colgan, decided to put on an end of term concert. Quite naturally, he asked Chris to come in and perform a couple of songs, but experience of the young Davison's past tendencies tempered his offer just a little. He warned him, "Now, Chris, last time you appeared you were really great and all that, but you do have to think of the other acts. So, just do two songs, ones that people will know, no Makey-Uppys, just a couple of Beatles' songs."

Chris, overcome with gratitude at being asked to perform, whatever the limitations, agreed immediately. But, of course, once he took the stage, there was no way he was only going to do two songs. Susan Colgan remembers standing in the wings, listening to him, and thinking 'This is really nice, this is great.' "I'd forgotten I was meant to go on next, in fact, I think everybody had... everybody, that is, apart from Mike. He was standing there, gesticulating wildly, almost begging him to stop. And when Chris did finish, everybody went crazy. He had just been so good..."

One of the songs Chris performed that night, for the first time, was one which even today ranks amongst his most sensitive. "I'd written this love song and of course I had to try

it out immediately. After the show, two girls came up and asked if it was one of my own. I told them it was, and they said 'Well, it was beautiful. It made us cry.' And I didn't know quite how to react. In a way, I was choked as well. At last, I'd got a reaction!"

The song was called 'Satin Green Shutters', and although there was no way of knowing it at the time, it was to prove something of a blueprint for Chris' later songwriting. *"Write down the words about how you cried... what would you do if your dreams came true?"* he sang, something which he still does today. "Say I wanted to write a song about separation. I'm lucky in that I've been very happily married since 1978, so I have to imagine what it would be like if... It becomes quite a process for me, I get terribly upset inside, but I imagine what it would be like, how I feel, what I would do, work myself up into quite a state, and then write it all down. Fifteen years on from that song, I was writing 'The Head And The Heart', about two people who go away for a weekend in the country to try and work out their problems... and of course it doesn't work. I know quite a few people who are in that sort of position, and I can imagine that I am one of them. From there, the whole scenario develops.

"And the real success for me is still having someone come up and tell me that I've got it right, that that is exactly how *they* would feel in that situation. I think it was that remark from those two girls which suddenly woke up in me the possibility that there was something to be had from my music. I took the whole thing a lot more seriously after that. For instance, I had a friend in the University who was involved in songwriting, he had a couple of records out in Ireland, which I thought was very impressive. But when he played me a couple of his songs, I immediately thought I could do better than that, as one always does. And I made up my mind to prove that. Meanwhile, another friend of mine wrote a musical, very much the Son Of *Hair*, which involved me writing and recording something like 21 songs over a very short period. Some of them weren't bad, actually, and that again awoke my interest. The musical never got off the ground, of course, but it was a start and I learned a lot about writing under pressure from it."

Another elaborate plot with which Chris became involved was a musical starring a future Irish disc jockey, Maxi. She was part of a band called Maxi, Dick and Twink, and Chris remembers, "It was the first time I'd been in a recording studio, albeit an eight track, and I was working with professional people, who'd been in the business a while. But they were happy enough to let me be the musical director for the day. It was an interesting experience, although nothing ever came from it."

"I remember him as a young man in the corner with a guitar, to whom everybody turned when they needed a melody," Maxi later recalled. "He seemed to be made of music, he had a totally natural flow."

Chris visited London fairly regularly during his time at Trinity, and on leaving, in the summer of 1971, he made his way straight back there. "I liked the idea of the music business," he says, "and it seemed to me that the only things you could do with a B.A. were become a teacher and get a diploma, or work in a bank. I'd been to a few interviews, more out of curiosity than anything else, and I'd been offered a couple of jobs in banks, but really, I couldn't face that idea, so I came to London and decided to give the music a go."

Together with two friends, James Morris — an aspiring studio technician — and Richard Fegen — a hopeful television script writer — Chris rented a house in South Wimbledon (Morris now co-owns the massive Windmill Lane recording studio in Dublin, Fegen wrote the acclaimed British TV series, *Chance In A Million*). "Richard and I were writing together, so we were always shut up in one room together," James says. "And Chris used to disappear into his own room to write his songs. He was extremely hard-working, although we didn't really take much notice of what each other was doing. When we were

together, off hours as it were, we never really spoke of what work we were doing."

"I was taking risks whenever they came up," Chris says. "I've often regarded myself as having been very lucky, but I did work hard. For instance, a friend of mine opened a hamburger restaurant, and he knew that I needed money so he asked me if I'd like to sing there, six nights a week. He offered me £2 a night, a hamburger and all the wine I could

Top Left: Sue and Paul Tullio's restaurant at Annamoe, Co. Wicklow, which is mentioned in 'A Perfect Day'.

hold. And so, every night I'd be sat in the corner of this restaurant, hunched over a microphone, playing background music to the customers. Every so often I'd play something they all knew, and they'd stop eating and applaud. Then I'd slip in a few of my own songs, and they wouldn't take a blind bit of notice."

The Makey-Uppy stuff received a better reception when Chris made his first concert tour, in 1972. He had become friendly with a local group, Horslips, and was invited along to

Left to right: Doug Flett, Glenn Morrow, Diane and Guy Fletcher in Topanga Canyon, Los Angeles, 1978.

support them on a short tour of their mutual homeland. Very much a traditional Irish folk band, proud of their heritage to the extent of waiting until St. Patrick's Day before turning professional, Horslips in 1972 were one of the biggest acts working the Irish circuit. Two hit singles, 'Johnny's Wedding' and 'Green Gravel', and a debut LP which became the fastest selling album in Irish rock history told only part of the story. Unlike other Irish bands — Thin Lizzy is a prime example — Horslips made a firm decision to break their home market first, and worry about the UK afterwards.

"It blew my mind to go from playing in a restaurant to playing in front of 2000 people seated at a concert," remembers Chris. "That was another key point in my life. I did a couple of tours with Horslips, I'd go back to the restaurant for my £12 a week, then go back on tour for £10 a night, and they (Horslips) were very good to me. One of the nice things about Ireland is that there's always a very strong sense of community. People are willing to help each other and if they do well out of it, all the better."

Despite the success of this outing, Chris still did not feel particularly ambitious. "I had the feeling that I could get on in the music business, but the idea of getting a recording

contract was light years away. As it turned out, getting the contract was essential, as much as is having two legs to run on. Because otherwise you're just limping along on one leg." In October 1972, Chris took his first steps towards growing that vital second limb.

A friend of the family, graphic designer Bob Williamson, another of those who spent their summer holidays at the castle, was a close friend of Doug Flett, the publisher and songwriter. With his partner Guy Fletcher, Flett had enjoyed hits all around the world. When Chris met with him, one of their compositions, 'Power To All Our Friends', was a hot favourite to become the British entry in the 18th annual Eurovision Song Contest.

"Doug and Guy were pretty hot songwriters," says Chris. "They'd had a number of massive hits — 'Power To All Our Friends' (as performed by Cliff Richard) only just missed out on winning Eurovision, Elvis Presley recorded three of their songs… it was all pretty MOR, but nevertheless, they'd had a string of hits and Bob Williamson, a friend, with whom I was staying at the time, invited Doug round for dinner one night specifically to meet with me."

It was Doug's birthday, and when Bob called to invite him over, he mentioned vaguely that there would be a few other friends around. When Doug and his wife arrived, there was, in fact, only one other person, "This very charming young man from Dublin, Chris."

As the evening progressed, Chris suddenly announced that he was a singer-songwriter. Doug was sceptical. He'd been in the music business "a few years at this stage"; it was a tale he had been told so many times in the past. "But Chris had been so entertaining, he was obviously a very bright young man, so I said 'Come on then. Play me some of your songs.' He had his guitar with him, so we left the table, took our cognacs into the other room and he sat down and played me four songs, one of which was 'Satin Green Shutters', and absolutely blew me away. I was thrilled, most impressed, which was the last thing I'd expected to be, or even wanted to be. My first thought was that he was unique."

Immediately he arranged for Chris to go round to the office he shared with Guy Fletcher, there to see what effect he would have on him. A couple of days later, Chris arrived, guitar in hand, and, in Flett's words, provoked exactly the same reaction from Guy as he had Doug two nights before. Doug had told Guy he had met someone whom he thought was really very special, at the same time trying not to present his partner with a *fait accompli*. "But I knew that Chris was very talented, very exciting, and I needed to hear Guy's opinion. And listening to his collection of songs, we believed he had a marvellous voice, presence and delivery. We signed him to a publishing

deal the same month as we met him, and started working with him."

Hardly surprisingly, Chris was overjoyed. He understood his own limitations, he was willing to learn and, regardless of the category in which he placed their music, he knew that in Doug and Guy he had teachers who were second to none. "He was very dedicated to what he was doing, and he did take what we told him very seriously. For instance, within weeks, quite literally, of our meeting, we were talking about his singing power. He had a great voice, very powerful, but we knew that he could be even more powerful, if only he would give up smoking. So I told him this, that he could increase his range by a couple of tones maybe. And he stopped smoking the next day!"

Nevertheless, Chris today looks back on those days with some reservation. "They signed me to a publishing deal, but they also signed me to a production contract with this company they owned called Egg Productions. And it was a fairly grim thing. Basically, what it meant was... at the time you're signed, no-one knows if you're going to be a star or not, but just in case you are, the contract gives them complete control over your services as a recording artist." Egg owned Chris' recording rights, so any record deal signed afterwards

would not be made with Chris directly, but with Doug and Guy. They then had their own contract with Chris, while he had to sign a letter of inducement, stating that if he parted company with Egg Productions (which happened two years later), he would still have his contract with the record company. In the meantime, he would get less than 50 per cent of any deal signed in his name; Egg got the rest.

Production contracts have for many years been recognised as part and parcel of the music industry. The arrangement would be a straight fifty-fifty split between artist and company, expenses and profits both. But if an artist is unknown, unsigned, maybe even unwanted, the chances of their being able to contribute financially towards setting the wheels of progress in motion are slim at the very best. The contract, in essence, simply stated that any money invested in an artist's career at the outset could be recouped once success is achieved and substantial royalties accrue. David Bowie had a similar agreement with his manager at the time of his emergence in 1972, and he was not alone.

The fact that such arrangements tend nearly always to break down, often acrimoniously, once the artist starts bringing in the really big money (usually because the

artist considers any debt to have been long since paid off) is testimony only to how quickly it is possible to forget that without that early attention and expenditure, much of which may well have taken place without the artist even being aware of it, the whole thing might never have happened in the first place.

Chris agrees with this, but adds: "Publishers often offered advances or weekly retainers to their clients (Elton John and Bernie Taupin, under contract to Dick James Music at the outset of their career together, are a case in point), and I felt I should have had some sort of weekly help. To this day I think it was unfair of those guys. It meant I had to go out and work when I should have been indoors, writing. Because that's what I needed to be doing."

Simply in order to keep himself from starving, Chris found himself having to make a living as best he could. The range of jobs which he took was staggering. "The first thing was delivering flowers to attractive young ladies in negligees at 10 in the morning. Then I got a job at a delicatessen, up at five every morning and driving down to Covent Garden to pick up fruit and vegetables, then across to Smithfield to pick up meat. I'll never forget the sensation of walking with a 40 lb turkey over my back, the head of the bird slapping against the back of my legs. In the end I just had to get away. I'd saved all the money I'd been able to, so I took off for about three months to write songs. Until I ran out of money again and had to go back to work.

"I'd never say it was wonderful living in a garret... it was bloody awful, I had no money, I couldn't enjoy London, and even though I was convinced that the path I was on was the right one, I decided I was going to give it a certain length of time and then quit. I just couldn't handle the thought of starving pennilessly for the rest of my life. My family were very good to me, they were encouraging me all the way along and every so often they'd send me the odd little gift of money to keep my head above water, but more often I'd simply survive as long as I could, then go to Ireland just to lick my wounds and recharge the batteries before returning to London."

That went on for a year and a half, and Chris, in his own words, was getting nowhere. "I was trying to write songs for other people, like The Hollies. I didn't have any personal identity at all, I hadn't copped onto that and I didn't, not until the autumn of 1973. By that time, I'd really had enough. I packed up all my stuff and just went back to Ireland, to the castle, to my family. And it worked. Living in a 12th century castle, something that has been standing for eight hundred years, makes one feel very insignificant in the wheels of time,

like a traveller, a short term passenger. It was November, these long, sad, dark, melancholy days, and I got this very strong sense that it was absolute bullshit trying to write for other people. I was the only person that I could write for.

"Although I've always been aware of contemporary music and fashion, I've always felt it's a dangerous thing to pay too much lip service to what's going on. If you want to create something unique, you have to create your own style first. And that's what I've tried to do, and in that respect I believe I have become different from the crowd. Of course I have influences. But when I start a new album now, I spend a lot of time in personal contemplation and reflection, talking to myself — not out loud! — and it's a very lonely business.

"It's almost impossible for me to sit down and deliberately write songs. They always sneak up on me, I'll think of a word and a song will just build itself around it. I believe in the ability of the subconscious, the creativity of the unconscious mind. All the creative writer has to do is lift the drawbridge and suddenly all the information you've gathered, all your heritage, all your tradition, is in there. I don't know how I do it, everybody has their own way. I like to just sit and relax and mumble to myself and suddenly it all comes out. But to reach this point of release can mean weeks of

agony, and usually does. The most natural songs come out that way. The ones that come from your inner emotions are the ones which work best, because they come naturally."

Living in a cottage on the nearby beach was a young couple from Virginia, writer Joe Gunnells and his wife Julie. Chris and the Gunnells soon became firm friends. "It was great being there," says Chris. "We all hit it off in a very mystical way. Joe and Julie were a great help to me, they really identified me to myself and we had a very inspirational time. I wrote a lot of material that autumn, and I'd sit there playing it to them. I'd reached the end of my tether, I was sick of London, I'd decided that this was it, I'd do it my way.

"There's a very mystical feel to a country like Ireland and with Joe and Julie's help I wanted to try and bring that through in my lyrics. I am influenced by the mystery and superstition of Ireland, I feel that Celtic melancholy very strongly. Those mists come out in my songs. When I go to the West of Ireland I get the shivers standing on the moors looking at the mountains on one side and the sea on the other. It's raining over here, the sun is shining over there and there's a rainbow somewhere. It takes me back to the dawn of European civilisation. It is magical, mysterious, it's a fantastic place. It's where the Atlantic Ocean meets Europe for the first time, a very melancholy place but sad-happy."

CHAPTER THREE

CHRIS RETURNED TO London in February 1974 and almost immediately things started to happen for him. At long last, the demos he was recording for Doug Flett and Guy Fletcher started to sound individual, so much so that Flett felt confident enough to begin approaching record companies. They had already made three tentative attempts to land him a recording deal, but it was the age old story: the companies liked the material, but it wasn't quite there, there was something missing. Doug Flett explains, "While his songs were packed full of great ideas, lyrics, terrific tunes, they lacked construction. He hadn't yet learned the art of constructing a song. They would consist of two good verses, a bridge, a chorus, another verse and another

times. It was all good healthy stuff, but finally Chris went back to Ireland and we didn't really hear much from him for a while. Then one day he telephoned right out of the blue and said it had all suddenly fallen into place. He understood what we'd been talking about, he said, and he'd got some amazing songs. And I could tell... I could just tell that it was all happening."

Chris caught the next plane back to London and the very next day was sitting in Doug and Guy's office with his guitar, bringing them up to date with his repertoire. "He sang four songs which absolutely wiped Guy and I out. We were alternately in tears and laughing, we were almost sick from laughter. It was so good. And we said then, 'Now you're ready'."

Immediately, Doug called Dave Margereson, the head of the A&R (Artists and Repertoire) division at A&M Records in London. The company had only just opened a

Dave Margereson

bridge. They were all very good, but they were disjointed. It was like having two and a half good songs in one. He knew he was good, we knew he was good, but it wasn't quite right — yet. And it was a very frustrating time for Chris, because he knew what we were talking about, it just hadn't sunk into his soul, he just couldn't make that special jump.

"And at the same time he was still going on about getting a deal. We hadn't told him about the companies we'd tried, therefore he was pressuring us about that as well, and we did have fairly big differences of opinion at

London office — Dave, in fact, was the first London-based A&R man they employed. Doug had already met him on a few occasions, and considered him to be a "very astute person." However, the main reason for making contact was Doug and Guy's friendship with Dave's boss, Derek Green. They had known him since his earliest days in the music business, when Green worked as a motorcycle messenger for Cliff Richard's London office. More recently, he had been working with Doug and Guy at Rondor Publishing, one half of a mutual appreciation society. Doug and Guy were convinced that with Derek and Dave behind him, Chris couldn't possibly go wrong. "A&M, in our opinion, was the best independent record company in the world," Doug enthuses. "And that is what Chris deserved."

Margereson had been at A&M only a short time when Doug Flett first approached. Prior to that, he had been working for Screen Gems, cutting acetates by Carole King and The Monkees, then for CBS, first as promotion manager (in which capacity he was at least partially responsible for a string of number ones for the company (Gary Puckett's 'Young Girl' and Fleetwood Mac's 'Albatross' among them), and then A&R, where he worked with Johnny Nash and, as part of the package, the then unknown Bob Marley, who was one of Johnny's writers.

"Derek Green had just taken over at A&M and he asked me to join him a few times, but I wasn't really sure if it was a good idea. We were born next door to each other, life long buddies, and I was nervous because of what it might do to the relationship. It's hard working for someone who's your best friend. As a matter of fact it turned out terrific. I was in the basement at A&M, Derek was on the top floor and I referred to my quarters as the engine room and when I called him it was always 'engine room to bridge…'. (Derek has since confessed that Dave's office was a simple corridor. "I just told him to keep both doors shut," he says.)

"Doug and Guy got in touch and their pitch was that I simply had to hear this terrific singer-songwriter they'd got on their books. So I asked them to let me hear some stuff."

1973/74 was not the best time for anybody to try to secure a recording deal. A world wide oil shortage had thrown the music industry into a panic — oil, of course, being a chief ingredient in the vinyl from which records are made — and in both Britain and America record companies were dismissing acts left, right and centre, trimming their rosters down to the bare minimum so as to preserve vinyl for those artists whom they considered deserved it the most… the major sellers. Anybody who suggested signing a new act needed more than a good ear for a tune; they would have to be able to back their decision to the very end — the end of both their protege's career and their own if necessary.

For A&M the crisis came at a particularly bad time. A relatively new company, flush with its first successes — The Strawbs, Hudson-Ford, Stealers Wheel and Rick Wakeman, in America The Carpenters, were all approaching the peak of their individual successes — and suddenly a government edict demanded they worked a mere three days a week so as to conserve electricity. Anyone breaking that regulation was liable to be

arrested. Schools closed down early, street lighting was almost non-existent, power cuts were commonplace. And in the midst of it all, Derek Green and his staff at A&M would sit in their offices working by candlelight. "We wanted to work," says Derek. "We simply couldn't afford to sit around for two days a week doing nothing. We had artists to break!"

"Quite what the oil crisis meant to the music business I never really discovered," admits Dave Margereson. "At the time you just accepted what you were told and it's only later on that you realise that whenever there is an excuse to maybe pay only 90 per cent of your sales or whatever, they use it. But we were never limited to the number of acts we could sign, any constraints were self-imposed ones. For my part, if I signed an act, I'd want to be involved with the project all the way through, it wasn't simply a matter of getting the band's signatures on paper, making a record and then going onto the next project. I used to follow it through all the way, if only to make sure that the fruits of my labour got the airing which they deserved."

Simply on the strength of the seven songs on the cassette he received from Doug and Guy, Margereson felt exactly that commitment for Chris. Almost immediately it was arranged for the pair to meet, and Chris knew that the occasion called for something a little out of the ordinary.

Doug Flett told Chris that Dave was coming down to meet him, and that he'd have to play a few songs, just him and his guitar. Chris, however, had other thoughts. If Dave Margereson was that important, he wanted to give him an important show. He wanted to have a lighting effect. Says Doug, "Now, this was all taking place in our office, which was a fairly large room, but there was no way we could do anything particularly extravagant. He knew how important this meeting was, I'd told him that it was a great record company, that it was the record company for him, but he just smiled and said 'leave it to me'."

Suspecting nothing, Dave arrived at the office, very mellow, very relaxed. Doug poured him a drink, then he and Guy sat down. "Chris will be with you in a moment," Doug said. Then he turned the lights out. And before Dave had a chance to say anything, Chris suddenly leaped out of the cupboard in the corner of the room, where he had been waiting, guitar in hand, singing. Doug turned the light on, "and Dave just collapsed. It took him totally off-guard, it completely wiped him out. And the whole thing worked out just wonderfully. Chris played for about an hour, and at the end of this Dave just sat there, and although it wasn't a comedy act, his eyes were red and swollen from laughing so much. We had such a great time, we were all so happy, we were all just aching from laughter, and Dave said, 'We've got to have this man!'"

"To this day I've never heard a singer, just a solo singer, sound as be-witching and enthralling as that," says Dave. "It just took the top of my head off, the power of his voice and everything he had to offer. I was immediately in love."

Dave remembers Chris playing most of the songs which eventually appeared on his first album, an impressive repertoire to which Chris adds, "lots of titles which no-one has ever heard, which I've never recorded. The one I started with was called 'Hot Barrel Hannah', about the sort of hard woman who would howl in the night and all the men would shiver, the kind of girl who could make a horseshoe curl. I was still into writing comedy songs in those days. 'Patricia The Stripper' was one of them and there was another called 'The Star Spangled Tangerine See Through Topless Trousers' which was quite a song.

"A lot of it was pretty duff stuff, although it seemed great at the time. It always got a terrific reaction. But I've never been happy

with the comedy songs. My lyrics are quite often a total reflection of my personality and it's strange that I cannot get the comedy side down as well as I'd like to. Songs like these work great once in a while, but I find it terribly difficult for the comedy side to come out properly. The only one which ever really worked was 'Patricia The Stripper'. I wrote it at the castle during that autumn, and the very first performance was a really grim affair. We'd had this cook who died of cancer and his two brothers came over from Wales to lay him to rest and afterwards they came over to the castle for a drink. I remember sitting there in the dining room at that same table which is on the 'Castle Walls' album sleeve, and someone asked me to sing a few songs. So I did, then I asked if they'd like to hear a funny song, and did 'Patricia The Stripper'. And everybody started howling with laughter..."

"He had some great comedy numbers," remembers Dave Margereson. "He used to do lots of different voices as well. There was a

great Rod Stewart take-off which he did on a song called 'What's A Nice Guy Like You Doing In A Face Like That?' But it was his ballads which really convinced me. They were very moving, they evoked a film script in a way, lovely little anecdotes. And he had a real purity to his voice, it was immensely powerful. His guitar playing was never that good, but it got him by. He was, quite simply, terrific."

Any nerves Chris might have experienced before he met Dave were immediately calmed by the reaction the 'show' received. Within just 24 hours, Dave had made arrangements for Chris to meet Derek Green, and learned from Doug and Guy what sort of arrangement they wanted to come to over a recording contract. He resolved there and then to sign Chris to A&M.

"I was in heaven," says Chris. "Believing that all you needed was a recording contract and suddenly you were a star..."

Derek Green

25

CHAPTER FOUR

"C
HRIS WAS SIGNED to us at a time when we were making changes in the way the record company ran," says A&M chief Derek Green. "I took over the company late in 1972, just at the time when the American owners were opening a London office. In the past they had simply been licensing the label to British companies and didn't have a London office, so the first thing I had to do was build an operation, appoint staff and so on. That meant trying to convince my old pal Dave Margereson to come and work for me. And again, this was the first time A&M had had a UK A&R director, meaning that although there had been British acts on the label in the past, most of their dealings had had to go to the American office and things had got a little disorganised. A lot of the old catalogue needed clearing out and Dave's role was to create a new roster of artists, of which Chris was one of the very first signings, the first artists to work with the new sales and distribution set up. (Andy Fairweather-Lowe, on the run from the ashes of Amen Corner, was the first).

With Dave already sold on the idea of adding Chris to the label's roster, the next step was to convince Derek. "Dave had been at the company for some time by then, stuck in his corridor, and he was constantly auditioning new talent. One day he called me and said he was really hot for this guy, so I told him to let me meet him. So Chris came in, he brought his guitar and sang his songs, in the corridor, to Dave and I. And my first impression was that he had a remarkable voice, truly remarkable.

"I was a bit nervous that he was perhaps more of a troubadour than a pop singer; I asked Dave if he was sure he wasn't the Noel Coward of Pop! And it worried me because he was so different; his songs were rather nice, anecdotal, little stories. And the rock business is not rather nice. So I was concerned. I think what finally convinced me was the song 'Turning Round'. I heard that song and I knew why Dave had been so set on signing him."

Nevertheless, Dave Margereson still remembers having to, "really push Derek into making the deal. It was not a cheap one, and there were times when I felt certain it wouldn't come off. It was a tough deal for him to make."

Derek, however, knew that his hands were all but tied. "Dave was sold. He wanted Chris de Burgh on the label and he wasn't going to settle for anything less. For my own part, you take a chance on your A&R guy; you wouldn't have taken him on if you didn't have faith in his judgement. I'd been very impressed with Chris, and I knew that if Dave was that keen, that involved in the project, then we would be okay."

"A&R is a very egotistical thing," says Dave. "I've never asked myself whether such and such an artist would fit into any particular mould. It's always been more important to pursue my own taste. If it appealed to me and it felt different to me and got me going, then I'd say 'We'll make a record of it and *then* try to make a hit of it.' I'm sure one is influenced by what is on the radio at the time, although Chris had very little in common with *that*."

Indeed he didn't. Compared to its immediate predecessors, the year of 1974 was fast shaping up to be one of almost startling mediocrity. The sudden rush of new faces (if not talents) that had begun in the summer of 1972 had fast dissipated. Now only David Bowie, Elton John, Gary Glitter and Mud survived with anything like their previous chart-topping invincibility intact. The reign of Marc Bolan and T. Rex was over; in their stead The Wombles emerged from the depths of Wimbledon Common to become the year's best selling singles 'artists'.

In terms of mass popularity, however, The Bay City Rollers stole the thunder from beneath even their furry little snouts. Elsewhere in the U.K., reggae pretended to enjoy a major breakthrough, but somehow forgot to release any records capable of living up to the press hyperbole which preceded them, and it was left to the power of television — Crossroads, Eurovision, Opportunity Knocks — and a sudden nationwide obsession with the Martial Arts to challenge the seemingly eternal chart residence of aged French balladeers, country and western singers and 'Y Viva Espana'.

Into this climate, even more unsuitable than any which had preceded it, A&M planned to plunge Chris Davison, one man and his guitar. And without any more of a masterplan than that which Chris was considering. Visiting Paul Tullio one night, Chris suddenly asked which he, Paul, thought would be the better name, Davison or de Burgh. "He was saying he wanted to change, and that de Burgh

had the right ring to it. I disagreed. I thought
Davison was a perfectly good name for him,
but he had already made up his mind. I think
my saying he shouldn't change was simply the
deciding factor. If I'd agreed with him about
de Burgh, he'd have been completely thrown."

Doug Flett sums up the incautious
optimism with which everyone concerned
viewed Chris when he admits, "I didn't see
him as fitting into any particular niche, I just
saw him as immensely talented. One wasn't
particularly cerebral about it, it was purely a
gut reaction."

The first move was to find a producer with
whom Chris could work. It was Derek Green
who suggested they use Robin Geoffrey Cable,
an engineer at Trident Studios. "At that time,
studios would become suddenly fashionable,
their engineers would become the hit
engineers. Trident was about the biggest
studio in those terms: Ken Scott was there,
he'd done a few David Bowie albums, now he
was working with Supertramp, John Antony
was there, he'd worked with Genesis and Van
Der Graaf Generator and we'd used him on
another A&M band, Nutz. So there was a buzz
about Trident. But more important, Robin
did seem to be the right person for Chris to
work with."

The album that Cable produced, 'Far
Beyond These Castle Walls', was released in
February, 1975. Many of the songs were
written the previous year in Ireland — 'Windy
Night' in particular owed its genesis to those
nights spent in the cottage, conjuring up as it
did the elements which howled around that
isolated house while the inhabitants huddled
up inside, knowing that something was riding
on the wind, but knowing not what it was.
The song conjures up images of Emily Bronte's
'The Visionary', the dark desolation which so
characterised her writing, the loneliness of
isolated farmsteads and the submission to
powers of the night. Contrarily, the cautionary
tale of the 'Lonesome Cowboy' was a scene
straight from a John Wayne movie, a little
maudlin perhaps, but as effective as it may
have been affected. And then there was the
lascivious 'Sin City', a romp through
degeneration which afforded Chris the
opportunity to fall into one of his repertoire of
different personas, on this occasion a lecherous
maitre d' escorting the young and the innocent
around a Pleasuredome.

It is rare for any artist to unleash such a
potent album first time around. For all its

On the beach in Rio de Janeiro where '(Flying) Turning Round' was a number one hit in 1975.

roughness, 'Far Beyond These Castle Walls' was a far more confident sounding record than it even had a right to be, considering Chris' lack of experience. And it has stood the test of time much better than it might have; not, perhaps, in comparison with Chris' later recordings, but certainly when placed alongside comparable albums of the same period. Quite independently of each other, several 'new' singer-songwriters were unleashed on the world around this time: the revitalised Russ Ballard, Joan Armatrading, Judy Pulver, Julian Brook... of them all, only Chris and Joan have lasted the pace, of them all, only Chris' debut still sounds fresh. Maybe it didn't boast the vitality of his stage show — Chris' natural talent for expressing dynamics with his voice alone was drowned beneath Robin Cable's well-intentioned string arrangements — but that swiftly became a minor consideration, especially for Chris, who has always seen recording and performing as two entirely different mediums.

"I was talking to Derek Green, some years on, and he said that the one thing which struck him about that first album, which was really unique amongst artists, was how thrilled I was about the way it had turned out. I was over-awed; it was a naive response, I think, to hearing my songs recorded. I was so amazed to hear how beautiful and serene and extraordinary the whole thing was... I was really pleased with it." Thirteen years later, he continues, "Obviously it sounds extremely dated — there's a lot of that talking stuff, which really grates on me, but...it was popular then. Stuff like 'Satin Green Shutters', 'Turning Round' and 'Goodnight', I think, are lovely songs, though.

"First albums are always an artist attempting to define himself, and I think I came off better than an awful lot of people. Looking back, there are the seeds of what I was going to do, 30 or 40 per cent of the album continued to be enlarged upon, even more possibly."

Chris and Robin Cable were very close throughout the sessions, Cable patiently giving Chris the opportunity to find his way around the recording studio, and to learn of the benefits which it could bestow upon him. He drew Chris into the actual process of recording, valuing his opinions, and giving him the chance to express what he meant in his own words. He also impressed upon Chris the benefits of working under pressure; they were doing two backing tracks a morning, a

phenomenal rate which both preserved the electricity of the material, and allowed more time for working on the performance itself.

The song which had so impressed Dave Margereson and Derek Green, 'Turning Round', was, not surprisingly, recorded for the album, and subsequently released around the world as Chris' first single. The beautiful 'Satin Green Shutters' aside, it was certainly the most suitable song on the set. Undoubtedly, they thought so in Brazil, where the song topped the national chart for over three months. The first Chris knew of this was when he received a telegram telling him he had been number one for the past 17 weeks!

"I got there for a promotional tour, smiling and shaking hands and not playing a note of music, and everybody knew me, it was quite astonishing," he recalls. And laughing as he remembers how, for a good three years after, English journalists still referred to him as "The guy who's big in Brazil", he adds: "Apart from 'Lonely Sky', which was the follow-up, and which did fairly well, I didn't have another hit there until 'The Lady In Red'!"

Dave Margereson and Derek Green both remember spending days trying to persuade Chris that the song which was to bring him that success had been mistitled, that it should have been called 'Flying'. "We were being very heavy on Chris trying to convince him of that," says Derek, "The word which you remember having heard in the song is 'Flying'. But Chris was adamant. I know we managed to change it for some territories (one of which was the UK, where it was released under the new title), but for the most part Chris got his own way."

Both single and album went on to dominate charts throughout Latin America, but elsewhere in the world, they met with little success... much to Chris' surprise.

"In my naivety and excitement I thought that first album was going to conquer the world," Chris explained later. "But in reality, the best thing that can happen to anyone is for that not to happen. If you have a number one straight out of the box, it has to be the hardest thing to live with if you're interested in a long term career. As it was, that album was a big hit in Brazil, Argentina, Guatemala and El Salvador, but — with no offence to those countries — their record markets really aren't that big. So although I had some success, I didn't have that same reputation to live up to as I would have had if the record had been a hit in Britain or America."

CHAPTER FIVE

I N NOVEMBER, 1974, Chris went out on the road in Britain for the first time. The billing on the tour was quite extraordinary; Supertramp headlined the show, with second billing going to a film of Mike Oldfield's acclaimed 'Tubular Bells' composition, previously screened by the BBC Arena show. And opening the show was Chris, a diminutive 26 year old with just his guitar and Supertramp's equipment for company.

His set was short, but memorable. 'Satin Green Shutters' and 'Turning Round' were nightly highlights, 'Patricia The Stripper' the perfect encore. The skill with which Chris recaptured the feel of the English country weekend which was the inspiration behind that song was quite stunning. "Everybody was wearing dinner jackets, getting up at six to go fishing, they were all terribly 'Haw Haw'. And I was sitting there, sipping my Pimms and watching the tennis, and thinking; 'I'm going out to dinner with a gorgeous singer, to a little place I found down by the quay.' I wasn't acually planning to do anything of the sort, but it seemed so appropriate."

'Patricia The Stripper' proved to be the perfect crowd pleaser — the critic from *New Musical Express* described it as "The funniest encore I've heard in ages". But despite the notices and reactions Chris received around the UK, there was little doubt as to who the real stars of the show were. 'Dreamer', only Supertramp's second single ever, was climbing up the British chart; 'Crime Of The Century', their third album, was being heralded as one of the records of the year, if not the entire decade — panegyrics which the passage of time has done nothing to invalidate. It was they who packed out the halls on that first tour — Chris was simply the lucky first recipient of the audience's pre-show munificence; night after night on that British tour the crowd would have rallied to Chris' cause long before his short set was over, long before the riotous encore of 'Patricia The Stripper' had reduced entire auditoriums to hysterics.

Like Chris, Supertramp had Dave

Margereson to thank for their present standing. The band got together in the late sixties, the plaything of a benevolent millionaire. But two albums recorded for A&M had done little for them, and when Dave joined the company, one of his first tasks was to assess the band's worth, and decide whether it was worthwhile keeping them on the roster. "I went to see them live, and liked them a lot. But then the band broke up, while they were touring in Norway, and it looked rather like that was it for them. But I stayed friendly with the two writers, Richard Davies and Roger Hodgson, and somehow we put the whole thing back together again, a communal effort."

The intimacy which became such an integral part of Supertramp's make up was one of the ingredients which made it so easy for Chris to slip into their entourage, while the infectious family feel of the entire package ensured he would not be left out in the cold by even the most partisan of audiences.

"Chris became our resident support act, really," says Dave Margereson. "It started off when A&M took over the Kings Road Theatre for a sales conference, we had Supertramp, Chris and another band all playing on the same bill together. It was set up basically to present 'Crime Of The Century' to all the executives and people from all over the world, and I really liked the way Chris and 'Tramp worked together, not perhaps as musicians, but as performers. The theatrical side of things. It was always important to me that the shows we put on didn't belong only to the headliner, that the support band didn't get ignored. And we did some terrific tours together."

Chris' first dates with Supertramp, little more than half a dozen shows in selected 'Tramp strongholds around the country in December, were a warm up for 13 dates in the New Year. He did not appear on them all; Steve Ashley, another solo singer-songwriter, opened the show in Preston, for instance. The January shows, however, featured Chris throughout, and as with the earlier outing, ticket prices were pegged at just £1.00 — and that despite the 'Tubular Bells' film having been replaced by another live act, Scottish duo Gallagher & Lyle.

Innumerable tales, mostly apocryphal, exist about Chris as a support act. One which has been substantiated, however, concerns his refusal to go on stage while there were still people coming into the theatre. The show would be scheduled to begin at 7:30, but invariably, Chris would be nowhere in sight. Peter Bowyer, the promoter, and Dave Margereson would be frantically running around looking everywhere for him, but the old theatres of England are like rabbit warrens, full of passageways and little corners, and Chris would be sequestered somewhere there... somewhere where he could see the people coming in.

Dave knew why Chris did it. He took his music very seriously, not because he personally thought it was better than anything else, but because he simply wanted people to hear it. How many times had he himself sat at a concert or a theatre and had his own enjoyment spoiled by late arrivals pushing down the aisle, tripping over bags and feet on their way to their seats? So he would wait, wait until everybody was settled, until they had removed their coats and rustled their programmes. At the time, such reasoning was seldom appreciated by aggrieved roadies. For every five minutes Chris spent offstage, it meant someone would have to cut their set that bit shorter. All the same, believes Dave Margereson, "He was fighting his own battles. And he was winning them."

"Chris in his mind was always a star," says Derek Green, continuing that particular tale. "From the day we met him he was a star, it was just that nobody else was aware of it at the time. But he knew. Therefore, when stardom came, it didn't change him in the slightest. He was a star then, he's a star now, the only difference being that more people know about it now than did before. So instead of behaving like the little guy Supertramp would take on tour with them because he was cheap, he behaved like he had some importance, with the result that if he hadn't been so much fun, and hadn't been so mischievous, he'd have been thrown off the tour long before. That business about hiding... he was on the tour primarily to interest people in taking their seats before Supertramp came on, they'd be in the bar and hear him and come out to see what was going on. But Chris didn't see it like that, he wasn't there to get people in the room, he was there to play to them once they were already there."

That was, perhaps, Chris' biggest fight, trying to persuade an audience to listen. People were going to the gigs primarily to see Supertramp. Perhaps a handful were curious to see Gallagher & Lyle, if only because of their earlier success as the songwriters behind McGuinness Flint. But it was Supertramp's crowd. For Chris to even walk out on those stages, just a little guy with his guitar, was an act of considerable courage. "Once the show is rolling, it's not so bad," says Dave Margereson. "Audiences do tend to rally round to a solo artist, *if he's good*, more than they do a band. But those first few moments, I used to watch Chris and I would wonder just how he ever managed to look so relaxed!"

Chris' nerves were certainly given a thorough testing on those early tours. Practical jokes have long been an intrinsic part of the touring life, and neither Supertramp nor Chris were loathe to live up to such a glorious tradition. His promotional stickers would be attached to toilet seats, something guaranteed to put Chris on the defensive. "If that's how you feel about me, then you're all a bunch of..." was a not uncommon response.

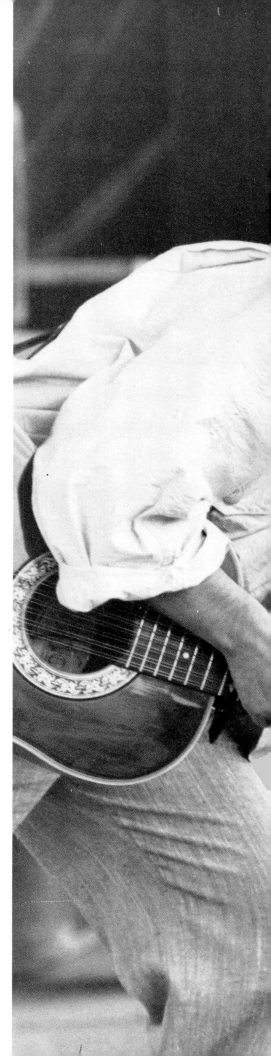

Top: Bob Siebenberg, Supertramp's drummer.
Above: Roger Hodgson of Supertramp.

One night in Vancouver, Chris finished his set and came off stage, only to be grabbed by members of Supertramp's road crew who had somehow laid their hands on a harness. They decided it would be a great idea if they could hoist Chris above the stage and leave him dangling there throughout Supertramp's set. Just the thought of him hanging there 20 feet above the stage, fists clenched in a real life enactment of the disembodied hands which grasp the bars on the sleeve of 'Crime Of The Century', had them in fits of laughter.

Fortunately, Dave Margereson did not share their humour. "I just went berserk. I managed to get there before they'd got him clipped up and really, I was ready to murder those guys. You cannot do that to someone in front of 60,000 people!"

On another occasion, Chris was onstage when suddenly Supertramp's drummer, Bob Siebenberg, appeared wearing a cloth cap and overalls and began sweeping up the stage around Chris' stool. "Chris always responded to those things very well," Dave remembers. "Afterwards he would most likely have wanted to kill the guys, but he always handled it well onstage. Because he can take an awful lot of stick, and I think it became almost tempting to Supertramp to try and find out what *couldn't* he take?"

On one memorable occasion, Russell Pope, the sound technician, cued up a cry of 'Albatross', lifted from a Monty Python sketch, and unleashed it full blast through the PA just as Chris reached a dramatic moment in one of his more poignant songs. In Bournemouth, a roadie walked onstage wearing a raincoat... and nothing else, flinging back the garment when he was standing level with Chris. Without losing a beat, Chris incorporated the sight into the verse he was singing. At another show, he came off stage at the end of his set, only to be thrust into a flight case and rolled out in front of the audience. Most people would have simply climbed sheepishly out and slunk offstage; Chris leaped out, singing another song! As Dave Margereson proudly recalls, "Nothing really threw him, and if one has to resort to purely physical overpowering, it doesn't really count. And Chris is not adverse to getting his own back, either."

Says Chris, "Supertramp were an incredibly arrogant bunch, and because of the way they liked to have the democratic process, the road crew turned out, at the end of it, to be even more self-important than the band. Everybody was flushed with success, the band was really happening, and they were really keen to make sure everybody knew it. And I think one of the reasons I came in for a lot of semi-hostile ribbing was the fact that I wouldn't lie down. I had to be really pushy to get myself onto the stage in the first place, and to get through to the audience. I had this attitude that if I was going to do this, the only reason was that half hour on stage, and I had to give it my best shot. And anybody who got in the way had to be pushed aside. And so, if the road crew started messing around, I would retaliate. I had to, I had to fight for my rights."

"Every tour I've ever done the support act gets a hard time," sound engineer Kenny (brother of Supertramp bassist Dougie) Thomson says. "In Chris' case, I think it really got up Supertramp's nose that an individual could go on stage in front of their crowd and really turn people around. And it's so much easier to play tricks on an individual than it is on a band. In all fairness, though, it did get rather heavy. Part of it was... you usually have a situation where a band has a support act, the tour ends, and never the twain shall meet. A different tour, a different support act. We did four tours together, and Chris almost got to be part of the package, which is one reason why he took more abuse than most people would get. But he's a very resilient character, he obviously got very upset, but he used to get his giggle back. He gave as good as he took... it's just that he was outnumbered by 30 to one."

Chris admits he did not enjoy the tours. "They were miserable. Part of them I enjoyed...I knew that I was sowing the seeds. But that first tour lasted five months, worldwide," Chris recalls. "And I grew up very fast, being given the most unbelievable shit, not only by Supertramp and their road crew, but also by the audiences. It was a real first blooding, and I came home knowing the size of the problem I'd taken on. I realised I would really have to hit it hard. I came home in bits really, but bloody determined to do it all my own way. There are a few tales about my getting booed off stage, but that, at least, never happened. I've never left a stage in my life.

It was a close thing, however. In front of 7,000 people in Montreal, Chris found his entire 25 minute set dogged by the baying of a pack of 30 or so local trouble-makers. Backstage, nobody watching could guess how Chris would react...and nobody was prepared for it. He finished his set, mild applause mingling with the barrage of boos, left the stage — and then returned to play an encore. "I'd had enough. I'd flown 2,000 miles across the Atlantic to be there, and there I was being booed. When I got backstage, I thought to myself, 'I'm going to do it,' and just went back out there. And I got the most unbelievable response!"

Such dogged determination simply had to pay off; it was surely no coincidence that when first a city fell for Chris' charms, that city was Montreal. "That was the first place," says Chris. "By the time my second album came out, I was playing 2,000 seaters everywhere else, and in Montreal I was headlining to 15,000, two nights. And no-one booed! It was ridiculous the way things exploded there. Eventually the album went triple platinum in Canada, 300,000 copies sold."

Charlie Prevost was working in A&M's Canadian press office at the time of Chris' first visit to the country. Already a staunch Supertramp fan, he was prepared to give 'Far Beyond These Castle Walls' a fair hearing, simply because of Chris' connections with Supertramp. However, he admits; "I thought it was one of the worst records I'd ever heard, although my boss at the time absolutely loved it. I'd talked to Dave Margereson, and in the course of my trying to do things for Supertramp in Canada, he told me about Chris, and how important an act Chris was for him. But when the record came in, I didn't know what to expect... I loved the graphics, but I really didn't understand the music. I'm not very lyrical, whereas Chris is, so that created a distance there, and I was far more into Supertramp's kind of music. But Dave told me Chris was coming in with Supertramp (their debut North American dates, following on from the so-called One Pound British tour), so I knew I'd get to see him. I found out later that A&M had really decided to get behind Supertramp on this tour, buying up tickets and underwriting the outing to the nth degree, and I think Chris was only included because he was inexpensive." Supertramp left Canada with their future superstardom seemingly imminent.

According to Charlie, however, "Things didn't look good for Chris. That night in Montreal shook him, I think... it would have shaken anybody. But later on, after the American dates, Supertramp and Chris came back to Canada and they played Toronto, a massive show. Chris was onstage, playing, and everybody in the audience was talking. It was like being at a coffee club, you could hear the audience talking while Chris played, but the moment he ended a song there would be the most rousing applause... it was major. And we couldn't figure it out at all. But we knew then that something special was happening."

Canada swiftly became almost a second home for Chris, at least in terms of his career. The French-speaking area was the first to succumb, just as it had done for Supertramp...the west of the country proved a little more troublesome, simply because it is so America-orientated. They get all the radio stations from Seattle, and they are incredibly well up on what is happening in the States. "Eventually, though, things took off for me there as well. I think part of the reason is that I always got on very well with the press. The first promo tour I did in Canada amazed me; I was used to the English thing, where there's the national radio network, the national newspapers. And of course in Canada, it's nothing like that, it's all local papers (even if

they are covering an area the size of England!), all the radio and TV stations are for one area only, and it was really tough. I did eight cities in 10 days and it the first time I'd ever done a tour like that on a major level. Someone would ask me a question and I'd answer the best I could, go really deep into things... I was like a zombie by the end of the tour. I'd never talked so much in my life!"

•　　•　　•

Born out of the frustration and anger which he had built up over five months of touring, Chris' second album was 'Spanish Train And Other Stories', released towards the end of 1975. Like 'Castle Walls', it was produced by Robin Cable. Unlike its predecessor, however, it saw Chris' influences and imagination taking over. One of Cable's greatest influences was Phil Spector, not in the sense that he wanted to emulate the American's 'wall of sound' technique so much as to stamp his own productions with a similar sense of personal individuality. It was a process which usually worked — his handling of Dana Gillespie's 'Weren't Born A Man' album (released the previous year) for instance, was exemplary. But the lashing of strings and orchestration which he applied to the songs of 'Far Beyond These Castle Walls' seemed somehow out of place. Dave Margereson perhaps best sums up its faults when he says, "It was a beautiful sounding record, but it never captured the effect of Chris jumping out of that cupboard."

"I think Robin approached the album more from an arrangement's point of view," says Derek Green. "The strings and the dynamics, rather than concentrating on the structure. At the very beginning, Chris had a slight commercial weakness, in that he found it very hard to create the right bridge in a song. He could come up with a hit verse and a hit chorus, but he couldn't find the bridge. And that would leave the listener a bit disturbed, because the song wouldn't flow properly. It would always take a few listens before it began to make sense, and in the mass market people didn't have the patience for that. So to compensate for that, Chris would go into his really powerful voice, to cover the fact that he hadn't found the right bridge. Within those limitations, I thought the album worked, but it could have been a lot more powerful."

'Spanish Train' saw Chris and Cable again struggling to overcome that weakness, this time by throwing all caution to the wind and letting rip with every musically pyrotechnic device they could lay their hands on. The result was an album of almost maniacal ferocity.

"I got home from the Supertramp tour hopping mad. And I knew that what I had to do was write songs which would grip people's attention when played by a solo artist. 'Spanish Train' is an almost frighteningly intense album, which is exactly how I felt. I respond very well to pressure — I don't like it but I can respond to it. I fight back, I receive bad luck and it flattens me, but then I get back up and I roar. And that is the sound of that album. The first album was critically well received, but 'Spanish Train' is still the one people come up and talk to me about.

"It's become something of a classic now. Even now, I don't think I'd change anything about it. It might be a little delicate in places, but it's outside of time and certainly outside of the music industry. It was done out of innocence, I think... the more you learn about the industry the more you lose in a way. I was very naive when I recorded that record, I didn't know how I should be doing things, I just went and did them."

To fully appreciate the power of 'Spanish Train', one has to transport oneself back to the time of its release, to a time before the techniques which Chris and Robin Cable employed almost out of innocence, were being quite cynically picked up by others, and utilised on any number of other projects. Long before the likes of Steve Winwood, Phil Collins and Peter Gabriel brought a kind of respectability, via their own reputations and talents, to that breed of music which is so often disparagingly referred to as Adult Orientated Rock, and which was then regarded as a peculiar anomaly halfway between 'Dark Side Of The Moon' and James Taylor, 'Spanish Train' took contemporary frames of pop sensibility and married them to traditional values which would normally have sounded distinctly out of place on the average Progressive Rock album. It was an album of distinct contrasts, bright lights and threatening shadows, which alternately raised the listener from the highest excitement to the darkest melancholy, naively manipulating the emotions with the same, devastating effectiveness as other artists might today spends weeks trying to gauge. Throw in the metaphorical kitchen sink, and hardly surprisingly, even today it is the standard by which both Chris, and his supporters, still measure his work; it is a record with which one feels either instantly at home, or forever alienated by. Chris has, since the release of 'Spanish Train', been accused — and not always unjustly — of recording Easy Listening music. 'Spanish Train', however, was anything *but* Easy Listening.

For 'Spanish Train', Chris delved deep into the Celtic heritage which burned so fiercely within him, reiterating the bones of tales set not in the urban chaos into which they were to be despatched, but in a time when life was gentler, where the elements of wonder and romance predominated. They spoke of a delight in wild, untamed nature, in the music of the woodlands and of a time when such things were remembered and celebrated, but no longer habitually lived by those who idealised them. He drew close to the Ossianic tales of Irish folklore, the poet Yeats' *Lovely apparitions sent to be a moment's ornament*, and it can be no coincidence that many of those particular tales took place in Connacht, the province of Chris' forefathers.

Ireland, alone of the five great Celtic strongholds (Brittany, Cornwall, Scotland and Wales are the others), has a vernacular

literature which predates the introduction of writing by several centuries. Indeed, no Western culture outside of Rome could claim so rich and well preserved a heritage as that of the Irish, nor could they point to so distinctive a tradition. Irish literature was a law unto itself, a complete reversal even of the values so cherished by the great Latin scholars, depicting a world where logic came a very poor second to belief, where *aes sidhe* walked side by side with mortal man, loving and living with him until they were defeated by the *Goedil* and condemned by that defeat to live amongst the shades, to cross over into the realms of popular mythology.

"From the earliest days," says Dave Margereson, "almost from the first time I saw him, I thought of Chris as a balladeer, in the best sense of the word and the oldest sense of the word. He is a story teller in song, a troubadour. I could see him trotting from castle to castle, Lord to Lord, singing his songs and being well received, well fed and well paid in doubloons and ducats. He could have been a minstrel at the court of some great feudal Baron."

In taking his cue from the oldest legends of his homeland, Chris was following in the footsteps of his earliest mentors, Horslips. They, for their second album in 1974, had taken *The Tain*, one of Ireland's greatest heroic sagas (and one which dates from at least the 4th century) and presented it to an audience which may not otherwise have been aware even of its existence. The difference was, while Horslips and the likes of Breton Alan Stivell, simply reiterated the faiths of the Celtic lands, Chris enlarged upon them, developed them in a fashion which did not so much borrow from, as give some continuation to, the ancient folk traditions. "I never took any interest in modern Folk Music," Chris admits. "I found

most of it unutterably boring — and unentertaining. I was more interested in the story-telling tradition." The songs he sang came directly from his own imagination, just as, centuries before, the songs of the minstrels and bards had come from their imaginations. 'Spanish Train & Other Stories' was not a folk album, but in adopting the mantel of the storyteller, Chris was a folk singer in the purest sense.

"Many's the night I've spent in pubs, listening to story tellers and fiddlers and the old folk tradition," says Chris. "It's all called Folk music now, but it is still the old tradition, the passing on of a story from generation to generation. It's a lovely tradition really, and it isn't only Celtic or Irish, it's in the European tradition as well, that same sense of melancholy. I think that's the key to all folk music... the sadness, the peasants working the land, the farming and the bad weather. It's a curious thing, like an awareness of your own mortality and the human condition. You're kind of elated, but you're sad as well."

Perhaps the most obvious example of this tradition at work was the album's title cut, 'Spanish Train'. The song took shape in Spain, where Chris was holidaying during a break in the recording of the 'Castle Walls' album. "I was on a train to Seville, going very slowly, and I was looking out of the window and was suddenly struck by the way the Spanish make divisions between fields, just a few gnarled, twisted pieces of wood. There was a line of them going up a hill and I thought 'God, they look like dancing skeletons.' A few minutes later we crossed a bridge over the Guadalquiver river and I just scribbled down, 'There's a Spanish train that runs between Guadalquiver and old Seville.' Then I had a vision of a train thundering through the night with the driver,

a skeleton, leering out of the cabin, his bones lit up by the fire in the boiler. That's what started it off, I just made the rest up as I went along on the train."

'Just Another Poor Boy' and 'A Spaceman Came Travelling', too, possess that same quality of startling originality and cosy familiarity which is at the heart of all great stories. The climax to the first song sees an obviously Messianic leader led away by soldiers who claim, "His public meetings were a danger to the State" — the parallels between this and the tale of Jesus' arrest are obvious, but nevertheless, it comes as no surprise when Chris tells how equally valid parallels were

drawn by black leaders in South Africa.

"In one area, they adopted the song as their own anthem," he says, adding that the 'Spanish Train' title track was actually *banned* in South Africa, the Pretorian government taking exception to the references to The Devil in the title track. For two years, it was released there as 'Lonely Sky And Other Stories', reverting to its original title only after A&M took the matter to the High Court.

In 'A Spaceman Came Travelling', Chris reiterates the Nativity, but does so in a way which owes less to the religious overtones such subject matter normally implies, as to the writings of Eric Von Daniken. Nevertheless,

Above: Truck driver John Rivett as 'Patricia'.

the song has since become what Chris affectionately calls a hardy perennial, reissued every Yuletide to bring perhaps a touch of unseasonal science to the Festive season. In 1985, it was featured on a special Christmas compilation album, rubbing shoulders with the likes of Slade, Wizzard, Wham! and Shaking Stevens, and immediately it found its way into another 1.2 million homes across the UK; the following year, a remix of the song scraped into the U.K. Top 40 for the first time, riding at least partially on the shirt tails of Chris' first British hit single, 'The Lady in Red'. In an interview with BBC television presenter Philip Schofield (better known,

perhaps, as a man who introduces children's TV programmes with the help of a gopher), Chris said, "I was sitting in a flat, in London, on a hot summer day in 1975, and I was mumbling 'de de dum dum dee, a spaceman came travelling', and then thought 'Why? What's he coming to do?' And for no reason at all, I started looking at the Christmas story as if Jesus had a visitor from outer space…"

Despite its intensity, and the impact which the record was to have on both his reputation and his career, Chris believes there is very little of himself in the 'Spanish Train' album, that he is simply telling stories and, as such, is no more in control of what the

characters do than would be a newscaster relaying the day's headlines. "It's very easy to get caught up in the superstar myth, on stage every night with thousands of people listening to you. But I am perfectly aware that what they are seeing is the person they have built from listening to the music, a totally different person. They think they know me very well, but that is not necessarily so. I build personas around songs, and simply act out the part. If they knew me as I am at home, I don't think they'd recognise me at all as the person they've built up from the songs. They certainly wouldn't take me as seriously as they sometimes do!"

One example of this role-playing is 'The Painter', described by Chris as "a bizarre little tune based around Browning's 'My Last Duchess'." Browning's greatest strength was his ability to conjure a moment out of time and present it as an entity in its own right, an excerpt from a lost play, perhaps, from which the audience is expected to deduce for their own pleasure exactly what happened before… and after.

In 'My Last Duchess', a stern, severe Italian princeling of ancient stock is entertaining his prospective father-in-law by guiding him around his picture gallery. One particular painting strikes the guest's eye.

"That's my last duchess painted on the wall, looking for all the world as though she were still alive," explains the host. *"I call that a piece of wonder, now".* And when the guest comments on the animation in the Duchess' features, he is told that *"the depth and passion of her earnest glance"* was not reserved for her husband alone, but for any man who paid her attention… particularly the painter, Fra. Pandolf. In 'The Painter', Chris contracts that scenario even further, and tells the listener just how the *"spot of joy"* came to be in his wife's eye in the first place… and how he cured her of it. *"And I hope it's the rope for that painter…"*

The flip of the coin was 'Patricia The Stripper', the in-concert favourite translated, surprisingly succesfully, onto vinyl. "That was an odd track," says Derek Green. "There was a lot of call for it to be released as a single right from the start, and I always found it a really difficult idea to get behind, because while it was the one track I was getting the most feedback about, I knew that if that was the way an audience was going to discover Chris, then they were never really going to discover him. If all they knew about Chris was 'Patricia The Stripper' then we'd never get to sell albums, they'd just be looking for the next 'Patricia'. I was forever having to over-rule the marketing people when they suggested putting that out as the first single, in the end a Radio 1 producer, Bernie Andrews, convinced us to go with it because he was getting so many requests for it. So we put the single out… and it didn't do anything."

*t*HE RELEASE OF 'Spanish Train & Other Stories' brought to a close one particularly, or at least potentially, turbulent relationship. Chris' contract with Egg Productions was up, and he had no intention of renegotiating.

Despite a regular annual advance of £4,000 from A&M, Chris was living on just £40 a week, of which £22 was immediately gone on the rent and rates on his mews flat in Bayswater (to which he had only recently moved, a glorious respite from the parade of friends' floors and sleeping bags which had accommodated him over the past year). The rest of the money was swallowed up by Egg. Now Chris was free of them, but even so, his dealings with the company were not over — Egg demanded, and got, a percentage on all future sales of both the albums Chris recorded whilst under contract to them. "No wonder it all ended bitterly!" Chris later remarked.

However, 1975 also marked the beginning of another, far more enduring, and infinitely more important partnership for Chris. Through his friendship with Paul and Susan Tullio, he had been introduced to Susan's sister, Diane Morley, back during his University days. Any hopes of a relationship developing, at that time, were stymied by a quite disastrous first date, which left both Chris and Diane feeling so uncomfortable that, at the end of the evening, they simply shook hands and went their separate ways. "It was a nightmare!" exclaims Chris. "We went out to this Chinese restaurant in Dublin, and the first thing I did was order a bottle of sweet Sauternes, under the impression that it was a dry white wine. Things just went downhill from there; the food was awful, the conversation was non-existent. I thought she was too quiet, she thought I was too pushy. We said goodnight at the end of the evening and didn't see each other again for another three years."

The pair met up again in Dublin, when Chris turned up at Paul and Susie's flat one night, while Diane was visiting (he was a regular guest, staying over on the couch even on Paul's wedding night!). Says Diane, "I had been in London through 1973, and I did try and get in touch with Chris, because I knew he was there as well, but it seemed that every

time I tracked him down there, he would have gone back to Dublin. Then he would return my call when he got back, and I'd have just left. We simply kept missing each other, and this went on for about two years."

Paul remembers one particular afternoon, from which point on Chris and Diane were inseparable. "Chris still had his smelly Renault 4, and one beautiful, sunny day we decided we should all pile into the van and go down to the beach for a picnic. There was just the four of us, Susie and myself, Chris and Diane. Chris had his guitar with him, and whenever I think of how the two of them got together, that's the afternoon I remember."

Packed up a picnic and set off for the sea
Taking all the back roads where no-one else would be
Me and you and Paul and Sue, how we laughed the time away
And we had such a perfect day...

I brought along my old guitar
And lying there beneath the stars
We sang all the Beatles' songs we knew
Lord, you should have heard those harmonies
When we did Nowhere Man, Let It Be...

Chris was about to begin recording the 'Spanish Train' album when he and Diane first started seeing each other regularly, and throughout the process, he kept in touch with Diane, inviting her down to stay at the castle when he was able to get away from the studio for a few days. When he visited Brazil, in March '76, he cashed in the proffered First Class air ticket in return for two Economy Class passes; later, when he took to the road once again, he asked her to join him. She agreed immediately, abandoning her life as a Temp. Secretary to take up a post which pitched her right into the front line. "Chris didn't have anybody actually working with him on those tours, so I was doing everything from catering to selling his records in the foyer after the show. Looking back, it seems such a simple way of doing things; there was just Chris and his guitar — he only had one in those days! No roadies, band members or anybody. It was great!"

Chris' 'entourage' remained a one-girl show until he hit North America, for a string of gigs with Gino Vanelli — "This big flash rock star with 22 synthesizers. He was being managed by an American named Richard Burkhart, who is an absolute gentleman. He

realised I had no management, so after taking care of me throughout America and Canada, he suggested working full time with me around the time I began work on my third album."

That was 'At The End Of A Perfect Day', released in 1977. "And just to prove that I had no sense whatsoever, I did an album of ballads, a la Cat Stevens. Because there wasn't a lot of feedback from the 'Spanish Train' album at that time, I didn't continue on that route. But I would say that 'Perfect Day' is pretty much my favourite of all my albums, especially songs like 'In A Country Churchyard' and 'Broken Wings'. It is also the one that has done the least business."

The whole feel of the record was one of peace, and solitude, and as Chris says, it contains some of his loveliest and most melancholic music yet. The title track, in particular, is quite stirring, the ghosts of old Beatles' melodies and Christmas carols haunting your mind as Chris sings of that special afternoon on the beach with Diane, Paul and Susie. It is difficult, though, to pick out any one song which epitomises the set, so wholly does it mesh together, the songs interwoven like some beautiful tapestry of romance and romanticism. The abrasive qualities which had so characterised 'Spanish Train', the rough edges which had given 'Castle Walls' the harsh sparkle which set the scene for its most intense moments, all were erased, to be replaced by a calmness calculated to shatter any preconceptions which the record's predecessor may have spawned.

In an interview with *Music Week*, Chris recalled how he used to enjoy Paul Simon's 'Still Crazy After All These Years' album. "And I thought then how I'd love to make an album where you could listen to both sides without having any dramatic or abrupt changes. That is what I tried to do with

'Perfect Day'. But following 'Spanish Train', which was a dramatic record, full of fire and drama, this one obviously disappointed a lot of people because they thought they were going to get more of the same. But I deliberately didn't want more of the same..."

It was A&M boss Derek Green's decision to invite Paul Samwell-Smith, once the powerhouse bassist with The Yardbirds, but now equally well-known for his work with Cat Stevens, to produce Chris' third album. The reasoning behind the decision seemed infallible; beginning with 1970's 'Mona Bone Jakon' album, Samwell-Smith had done much to harness Cat Stevens' original naive, almost folky charms, and streamline them to the requirements of a major audience. Their most recent project, 'Buddah And The Chocolate Box' had reached number two in Britain (to be held off the top spot only by the Bay City Rollers); in America, — where Stevens was contracted to A&M — 'Oh Very Young' and 'Another Saturday Night' had both breached the Top 10 singles chart. Derek admits he visualised Samwell-Smith working similar magic on Chris. And with Dave Margereson still tied up with Supertramp, Derek took it upon himself to plan out the next stage of Chris' career. "I always felt the best way to sell Chris was to emphasise the soft, romantic side. And Chris was quite happy to make an album of that kind, so although he kept telling me that he could do rock, I thought I was being very commercially orientated and that we would be able to promote his softer side a lot easier. Paul struck me as being perfect for that. I knew he had the sensitivity and the taste to make this an exquisite album."

"I've always had interesting associations with my producers because I believe that personalities should not enter into what you are working for, so that means I am never one

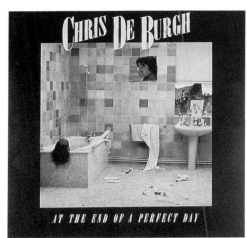

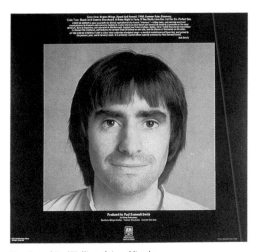

Top: Sue and Paul Tullio on their wedding day, with Chris and Diane, November 25, 1978.

to hold back on my feelings and we get into exchanges of opinion," Chris says. "I don't mind losing an argument as long as my side of it is given a fair hearing, but I have to put up a fight. Paul was not an easy person to work with because he was the opposite, he didn't put up much of a fight. I'd say, 'No you're wrong', and he'd say, 'OK, I'm wrong'. And I think that as a result of that, the record may have been a little softer than I might have wanted it to be. But there is certainly stuff on it that I still love to this day."

Immediately following the album's release, Chris went out on tour with Supertramp. By now, both his stature and that of the main attraction had grown to such an extent that only massive stadia could possibly hold their audiences. 'Tramp's most recent album, 'Even In The Quietest Moments', may not have been received with quite as much reverence, from public and critics alike, as its immediate predecessors, but there could be little denying that they were still one of the most exciting, and adored, live acts on the circuit. Similarly, Chris, although his following may not have been quite so widespread as Supertramp's, was at least well known enough that every venue on the itinerary was selected with his audience as much in mind as that of 'Tramps.

It was with this at the forefront of his own preparations for the tour that Chris realised the time had come to finally leave the one-man, one-guitar act behind him, and look instead towards a full band production. It was not a move which he embraced wholeheartedly; Derek Green remembers him as being "very resistant" to the whole idea. "It wasn't only for musical reasons either. Unlike a lot of people, Chris was smart enough to know that it was going to begin working out very expensive taking a band around with him, and he was scared, I think, of incurring that sort of cost. It was mainly Dave Margereson's bluster and bravado which finally convinced him that it was worth making the investment financially. It was the size of the venues he was now playing in that did the rest."

But still Chris was unsure, especially when he looked back on some of his past accomplishments. "The moment that stuck in my mind was something that happened when I did the tour with Gino Vanelli. We arrived in Montreal, his home town, to play in front of 9,000 people, and there was just me and my guitar. By that time things had really taken off there; I sang all the 'Spanish Train' album, which went down fantastically, and went back for three encores. I finished with 'Hey Jude', and had the whole place singing along with me. The reviews the next day were phenomenal, 'Chris de Burgh blows Gino Vanelli offstage', that kind of thing, yet all I had done was hold people's attention for 45 minutes, but if you can do that, just you, that is the most exciting thing (it also helped that Chris spoke French; local hero Vanelli didn't).

"It's the reason why I still play a few numbers entirely alone. I played to 35,000 people at a festival in Basle in 1985 and there was total silence for one of the songs. It was the most thrilling experience. But although I knew I could do that, I also realised that the larger a venue, the more need there would be to put on a show that people could see. One little guy with a guitar at the other end of a stadium simply wasn't what I wanted them to remember. So I put the word out that I was looking for a band and this guy knocked on my hotel door and introduced himself — Glen Morrow, the keyboard player — and said he'd heard that I was looking for musicians."

"He told me I was too tall, but he'd take me anyway!" remembers Glen, a genial Canadian who does, indeed, dwarf Chris. "I'd heard from a friend that he was looking for a band — I'd never actually heard his music before, but I went out and bought his latest album the day before I met him, learned the keyboard parts, and took it from there. We got one of Supertramp's roadies, Ken Alladyce, in on guitar, and with just the three of us, it gave the show that added visual impact it needed, without detracting from the original music."

There was still room for some improvement, however, and having taken the

Above: Jeff Phillips and Glenn Morrow, the original members of Chris' band, in 1977.
Left: Jeff Phillips, Ken Allardyce, Chris and Glenn Morrow.
Far Left: Ken Allardyce — the only known photo of the Flying Fist Band.

plunge, Chris wasn't adverse to going even further. During his tour with Gino Vanelli, Chris found himself being assisted more and more by one of the headliners' roadies, Jeff Philips. When Jeff turned up as Supertramp's drum roadie, on the new tour, and picked up where he had left off troubleshooting for Chris, it was not long before he, too, was offered a place in the live act. In September, he made his debut as Chris' drummer in Hamburg, the first date of the Supertramp European tour. And it was a mark of just how much respect the headliners now had for the plucky little chap who simply *wouldn't* go away, that, besides borrowing Supertramp's roadies, Chris was also able to call upon two members of Supertramp themselves to play along with him: guitarist Roger Hodgson and, occasionally, saxophonist John Anthony Helliwell, heavily disguised beneath caps and upturned collars.

"For all the abuse he got, it was a very much a family set-up, between Chris and Supertramp," says Kenny Thomson. "And I think it all came together because Chris just wouldn't quit. He'd take all the abuse and just come fighting back. He was accepted then, and Supertramp just did all they could to help him along in his career. I think now they're now quite shocked at how well he has done; he is, in fact, even bigger than they are, now (one particularly enduring joke between Chris and 'Tramp is the standing offer for them to team up once again for a tour...with Chris topping the bill).

This line-up endured for a little under a year, before a full time bassist, Ian Ellis, was recruited. The Flying Fist band was formed.

*t*HREE YEARS years previous, Dave Margereson had taken over the reins of Supertramp's career, shortly after the release of 'Crime Of the Century'. "I was looking after them almost on behalf of A&M. They were the in-house band in a way, and I think I brought to the project that feeling of having a common aim, of not needing a big-stick manager and so on. I had sent them out looking round what were then the big boy managers in London, and they came back and said 'Well, we've seen them all and to be honest, we'd like you to do it'. So I had a few sleepless nights over it because I was in a way the number two at the company, I had a very rosy future ahead of me at A&M, but I went for it anyway."

Dave joined Supertramp for the recording of 'Crisis — What Crisis?' in Los Angeles (from whence he still oversees the empire which his company, Mismanagement, has since become) and then accompanied them out on tour. "And although I was no longer anything to do with A&M, I still made sure that we used Chris an awful lot. We took him through Canada, America, many tours of Europe, and I used to get a bit berated by Supertramp themselves, wanting to know why they were out with him again. And it was really because I believed in him so much, and also because his set-up was very simple. Knowing how fussy Supertramp were about their equipment, it made things so much easier from an organisational point of view. Then, when things fell apart between Chris and Richard Burkhart, we were up in Montreal and Chris asked me if I'd be interested in managing him as well."

"It was during the English leg of the 'Quietest Moments' tour," remembers Charlie Prevost. "I was talking to Chris and I said, 'You know, your American manager's the pits, because people don't know who you are. They don't even know you're the opening act on the tour. Dave Margereson signed you, he's stood by you, you should really consider Mismanagement representing you."

Chris had already had thoughts along the same lines. "Richard was great, he knew my potential. But apart from his wife working for an airline, which meant he could fly in and out of London all the time on Delta, he couldn't

really do anything for me in Europe. He was great in America, but that wasn't the place that was happening for me at the time. So we parted on amicable terms, and I went with Dave Margereson."

For Dave, too, the move was logical. Supertramp were off and running, and Dave had built up an impressive entourage of people around them: road crew, electricians, designers, two sound engineers (Russell Pope and Kenny Thomson), tour manager Charlie Prevost and, overseeing it all, Dave and his first wife, Cass.

"We had a team in place, very good people who were terrific to work with," says Dave. "But I didn't know what I was going to do with them once the tour was over. Because Supertramp used to take an incredible amount of time between records. It was two years between 'Crisis...' and 'Even In The Quietest Moments', their next album. Do you just smash the team up and go away? We didn't do it with the road crew, for the most part they'd been together so long they were part of the family. And I didn't want to do it with the administration side. I had a big animal, a hungry animal. I wanted to throw it some more meat..."

Kenny Thomson joined the Supertramp crew shortly before the release of 'Crime Of The Century'. Working for the British Lion film company during the last years of their existence, he first heard the band whilst on a day trip to London from his native Glasgow.

"I went down to the Marquee to see Blodwyn Pig and Supertramp were supporting. Later, when their first album came out, I rushed out to get a copy, got home and played it to my brother Dougie, saying what a great band it was. He hated it! And two years later, he was a member of the group. Then when I left British Lion, I started work for Supertramp for £12 a week," he remembers, adding that his involvement with Chris grew naturally, simply, from nothing more than his nightly proximity to the singer. "In a way, I forced myself to become involved with him, it was simply the response to sitting there every night watching this guy flying in the face of absolute adversity, saying 'Sod the world, I'm going to do it anyway'."

Kenny joined the management in 1977, but throughout has retained his position behind the mixing desk. "Every show Chris has done since then, I've been there screaming at him. And that is a great position to be in if

*Above: Chris, Diane, J.P. Guilbert (A&M Canada) and friend in Montreal, October 1976.
Right: Noel D'Abo, February 1979.
Top Right: Chris, Diane and the band in Winnipeg at the end of the 1977 Canadian tour.*

you want to study how his career has exploded. We started off in Canada, where it was all theatres; six months later we were back playing the Montreal Forum, which is 17,000 people. That show was one of the highlights for me... at the end of it, everybody in the audience was in tears, and when the house lights came on, nobody moved for 20 minutes."

For Dave and Kenny, the first opportunity to work directly with Chris in a managerial context followed the Supertramp tour. 'At The End Of A Perfect Day' was the first album Chris had made upon which the responsibilities bred by the need to entertain an audience were a cause for consideration. Whereas 'Castle Walls' and 'Spanish Train' were both conceived at a time when Chris could be forgiven for thinking nobody was really concerned with what he was doing, 'Perfect Day' was to bear all the responsibility for continuing both his Canadian and his Latin American fame. Regardless of the quite dramatic shift which the record represented, however, its reception was at least kindly, not only in Canada and Brazil, but elsewhere around the world as well. But it sold very poorly in the United Kingdom, however, and that despite the full corporate muscle of A&M coming down behind it. Every year, it seemed, the company had gone all out to break one particular artist as a major new star. In 1972 it was The Strawbs, in 1973 Hudson Ford. Supertramp and Joan Armatrading followed. 1976 was to be the year of Chris de Burgh.

"The album, when it was completed, was everything I had hoped it would be," says Derek Green. "It really gave me a chance to sell Chris to the market. So I geared up a huge marketing campaign to push it. Now, when you do that sort of thing there is always the risk that you're going to frighten people off, that the selling is going to be too hard for

them. And this was one of those times. The timing was completely wrong, and I still believe that, if anything delayed Chris' final acceptance in this country, it was that we pushed him too early. I should have waited."

A headlining British outing was set up, with an all-out media onslaught to prepare the way for it. The gregarious Charlie Prevost was placed in charge of the operation. "Dave Margereson's exact words were, 'Whatever it takes, break the act'," remembers Charlie. "The sales in Canada were very big, and were encouraging everybody involved that Chris was an act that could happen. And by this point, I had started to develop a lot of respect for Chris... I'd been joining in with the abuse committee on those early dates as well, but I really admired the spunk of any guy who could go in front of an audience that wanted to see Supertramp without any support.

"He would walk out there, and he'd play his heart out, he really would. And I don't think I was the only one who was impressed by the way he did it. There was the way the band formed around him from Supertramp roadies; there was no budget, they just wanted to work with him. And it was a tremendous time."

Just as Dave Margereson knew he would, Charlie quickly mapped out a quite monstrous campaign to back up the tour, printing up literally hundreds of thousands of stickers, posters, flyers, all showing Chris' face — that was the angle Dave wanted him to go with, the face of Chris de Burgh.

The tour coincided with the release, in England, of the first of the *Star Wars* films, and the endless queues outside cinemas proved a fertile hunting ground for Charlie, Kenny Thomson and their co-conspirator, promoter Noel d'Abo. "We drove all through England handing out tickets and posters and records to everybody in those queues." At a time when local councils had really begun to crack down on unauthorised bill posting, the threesome decorated the entire country with pictures of Chris; in Manchester, Noel obliterated a police bulletin board, and Kenny Thomson well remembers how almost every night he would arrive at a venue, there to be met by policemen searching for "A Mr. D'Abo," unaware that the felon had long since moved on to terrorise another town.

"We put stickers on windows everywhere," says Charlie. "We got chased by the police in Brighton, we were nearly arrested in Bournemouth for disturbing the peace... basically what we were able to do, without anything more than a little weekend airplay on Radio 1 and a tiny bit of daytime play on Radio 2, was to sell out the Chris de Burgh tour. It wasn't easy — I remember a mad cab ride through London trying to catch the 10.15 train from Paddington Station, which everyone had thought left at 10.50. But by every trick known to man, we managed to sell out every gig on the tour. People in England weren't used to being promoted in this way, so they reacted. They wanted to know what all these crazy Yanks were doing running around being loud and extravagant."

"Charlie would talk to anything that moved," Kenny remembers. "He would go into retail outlets and spend an hour and a half talking with the staff about Chris. He did a lot for Chris, and while the record didn't particularly do anything, Charlie did establish that Chris could be a success in Britain as a live act. He was literally pulling people off the street and into venues. The street profile we had through his work was so high..."

For all his work, though, Charlie admits that he and Chris had their rough moments. "We are both very headstrong, me perhaps a little harder... I was rude to Diane, more in the heat of battle than anything else, but things like that didn't make life easy for us. I always thought he was a great talent, but we were never close. I was always just the promotions man, another part of the organisation. When I was at A&M he would come into the offices and charm all the girls, but I was just another businessman he had to deal with. And really, once that British tour was over, I didn't see much more of him for some years."

Chris' own recollections of that tour are somewhat less positive than Charlie's. Having headlined in his own right elsewhere around the world, particularly in Canada, he was somewhat unprepared for just how much leg work would be required to make the British tour a success. "Some of the gigs were okay, but others...we had to give away tickets."

●   ●   ●

The battle for the city of Acre was over. For almost two years the Crusaders had been besieging the city, not until they were joined by two new arrivals; Philip, King of France and his prospective son-in-law, the English King Richard, did the tide turn truly in their favour. The Englishman was not yet Richard the Lionheart, he was Richard the Ruthless, a man without fear, without mercy, without sympathy. Since their arrival, the Kings had amazed their men with their cunning, outwitting both the pagan Saracens and each other as they vied to be first through the city gates. The Saracens would have been beaten long ago had they not been barricaded within so strong a citadel. And now they had fallen, now Richard had exacted the retribution he felt the Saracens owed him for such a bloody, wearying siege. And now the victorious Crusaders were on the march again, to Jaffa. But Saladin, King of the Saracens, was waiting for

him. Arsuf stood not far from the ruined Roman city of Caesarea, wooded hills rolled down to the sea here, it was the perfect place for an ambush. But Richard was forewarned. He had studied the area in advance, he was well aware of the dangers Arsu might present. On September 7, 1191, he drew up his troops in readiness for the attack.

At 9 o'clock the Saracens burst from the woods like an apocalypse, an endless crescendo of gongs, shouts, trumpets and horns, of swarthy Bedouins and powerful Nubians already savouring the taste of victory and the smell of Christian blood. Then came the cavalry, so numerous that you could not see the ground, the dust so thick you could not see the sky. They charged, the Crusaders countercharged. Richard was exuberant; for him, endurance was everything. Back and forth he rode, Fauvel, his mount, sweating blood beneath him as he shouted commands, slashing at the foe and watched as his

men pushed first through the infantry, then the cavalry and finally into the woods themselves. The Saracens were a disorganised mass before them, running for their lives, heedless of the injured whose screams were the backdrop to the flight, whose lifeblood stained the earth beneath them.

One soldier, an Englishman, had attracted Richard's attention. Wherever the battle was fiercest, the bloodshed heaviest, this man was there, whirling like a dervish, cutting here, slashing there, thrusting somewhere else. The King rode over to him and enquired his name. "DeBurgh", came the reply. Then Richard knelt down and dipped his finger into the blood of a dead Saracen, a nobleman or perhaps a King. And with his finger he traced the outline of a cross on the sword of the man standing beside him. "Let this be your crest, then, wear it proudly in honour of all you have done on this most Holy of Crusades."

The family arms of the de Burgh family, to this day, are a crimson cross against a gold background, the motto *A Cruce Salus*. In the top left hand corner of the shield stands a rampant lion. Above the shield sits a cat. Family tradition has long told how Richard the Lionheart gave Baldwin de Burgh the right to call those arms his own, an honour which placed him high above the myriad others for whom the cross represented only their right to fight, for all that they held Holy, in the armies of England, of France, and of the Flemish lands, and how those arms replaced the symbol of Hubert de Burgh, an arrangement of lozenges. Perhaps Richard was aware of de Burgh's background, his illustrious ancestry which could be traced back to the time of Charlemagne and the family of the first King of Latin Jerusalem. The red cross was the emblem of the French armies — the English had taken the white cross, the Flemish the green.

"I have always felt particularly drawn to that period of history," Chris says. "The song 'Crusader' was my attempt to set down all I felt about the period. I didn't set out to write about the Crusades — the first lines came out of nowhere, and I had to figure out what the story was about."

"What do I do next, said the bishop to the priest,
I have spent my whole life waiting, preparing for the feast
And now you say Jerusalem has fallen and is lost
The King of heathen Saracen has seized the Holy cross"

Chris admits that historically, he took liberties. But the atmosphere of 'Crusader', by far the longest song Chris has yet committed to vinyl, could scarcely be faulted. The passion, the faith, the sheer belief of those men, who had been prepared to leave their homes, their families and even their lives, for the sake of a land which they knew only through the scriptures was all there. This, together with the corruption of those beliefs and high principles, which was as instrumental in the collapse of the Crusader kingdoms, as was the abandoning of such pettiness on their own behalf, the pivot upon which the Arab fortunes were reversed.

Then the Fool said, Oh you wise men, you really make me laugh
With your talk of vast persuasion and searching through the past
There is only greed and evil in the men who fight today
The song of the Crusader has long since gone away

The whole feel of the 'Crusader' album was one of excitable melancholy, tempered and strengthened by a certain timelessness best illustrated by the modern-day woodcuts which illustrated the inner bag. Just as 'Spanish

The 'Crusader' video.

Train' had been steeped in an awareness of heritage, both physically and spiritually, so 'Crusader' was a living tableau of a half-forgotten world whose values were encapsulated into the lyric of the closing 'You and Me':

I'll lead you through the ancient halls and stories of the past
And the many ways of loving
And when all is said and done, there is only you and me
You and me

Even without dwelling on their individual subject matter, the songs exuded the scent and sense of a world lost to the past, a world inhabited by old fashioned dancers dreaming of music halls, and sad farewells postponed in order that we can keep living together before everything slips away. Yet at the same time, everything was so alive and vibrant, filled with the roar of aircraft and the babble of television, almost drowning out that same plea for calmness whose echoes can be heard all the way back to the opening song on 'Far Beyond These Castle Walls':

Somehow he knows he's got to try to hold on,
somewhere she's crying for him, hold on...

'Crusader' was an album of hope; hope that the old world wasn't lost forever, hope that the values it once embodied still held good… and hope for the future.

On November 25, 1978, the 'Crusader' sessions still in progress, Chris and Diane were married, in Dublin. Chris flew back from London the night before the ceremony, enjoyed a three day honeymoon, then made his way back to England.

"It took me three years to propose," Chris admits. "I was completely knocked out by her right from the start, but I didn't think it was fair to ask her to marry a struggling musician who didn't even have a home to his name!"

It was for Diane that the key song on the album, 'Something Else Again', was written. Even more than the epic, four part title track, this was the heart of 'Crusader', a breathtakingly eloquent song, astonishing in its stark simplicity. Like Eric Clapton's 'Wonderful Tonight', its closest musical antecedent, and six years later, Chris' own 'Lady In Red', it minced no words, its sentiments were pure and direct.

All the nights I've ever known are waiting in her eyes
Sparkling like the silver, brimming like the wine
Other lovers laid me down, took my breath away
But this woman, she is something else again

"Diane has always been a great stabilising influence on Chris," says Paul Tullio. "If he ever comes back from a successful tour, behaving a little too boisterously, she very quickly brings him back down to earth. They are both on a very similar wavelength, especially when it comes to practical jokes; in fact it seems their relationship is based around deep affection and playing tricks on one another. She also encourages him to do it to other people, I think because he's had more practise. One of his favourite tricks is making hoax phone calls, using strange voices. He can keep it up for ages, and it's particularly infuriating for Susie and I, because we have a restaurant here, and there are always people with strange voices calling up…"

CHAPTER EIGHT

USICALLY SUCCESSFUL though it was, Chris was not content with 'Crusader'. And while it was, in reality, many miles removed from the world in which he and his audience moved, the reason for his disquiet was present almost everywhere he looked. Although he prepared for the album from a new, temporary, base in Los Angeles, living for four months in Topanga Canyon, and rehearsing every day with Jeff, Ken and Glen at Mismanagement's own studio in the city, he never lost touch with what was happening at home. And Britain, in the last quarter of the 1970s, was in the grip of a musical upheaval unknown since the 'Glam Rock' era whose power Chris had defied when he first courted the attentions of the marketplace six years previous.

Punk Rock was an alarmingly powerful antidote to the excesses which had been strangling the music industry during the seventies; it was also constructing a very broad divide between the adherents of the many musical genres competing for the same marketplace. You were either 'In' or you weren't… and Chris had already showed the world where he stood when he sent A&M chief Derek Green a telegram of support the morning after arch-punks The Sex Pistols were

dropped from the label just eight days after they had been signed. "Don't worry, there is life after the Sex Pistols," read his cable.

In its own way, 'Crusader' was a courageous record for Chris to make: the fire and drama of 'Spanish Train', the sensitivity of 'Perfect Day' were now joined by a third quality, a power and energy which hinted that, fiery detractor though he seemed, Chris had been affected by what was going on around him much more than he was prepared to admit. Just as Pink Floyd, Yes and The Rolling Stones had shown their grudging awareness of the new powers in pop by delivering their most convincing albums in years, so Chris had seemingly taken a step in the general direction of the new regime as well. The album's subject matter might have been far removed from the angst and anger one normally associated with Punk, but its energy and sense of personal conviction could not be denied.

"Right from the start I always felt I was away from the mainstream, and only history would be able to tell just how Punk would affect me. We've all seen now that it was a great energy kick, and an important source of adrenalin. But it was all over with so fast, and so many bands, the top-line ones, virtually ignored it, they just kept on doing their own thing, and they've survived a lot better than most of the groups who were supposed to be replacing them. I was aware of what was going

Opposite: The 'High On Emotion' video.

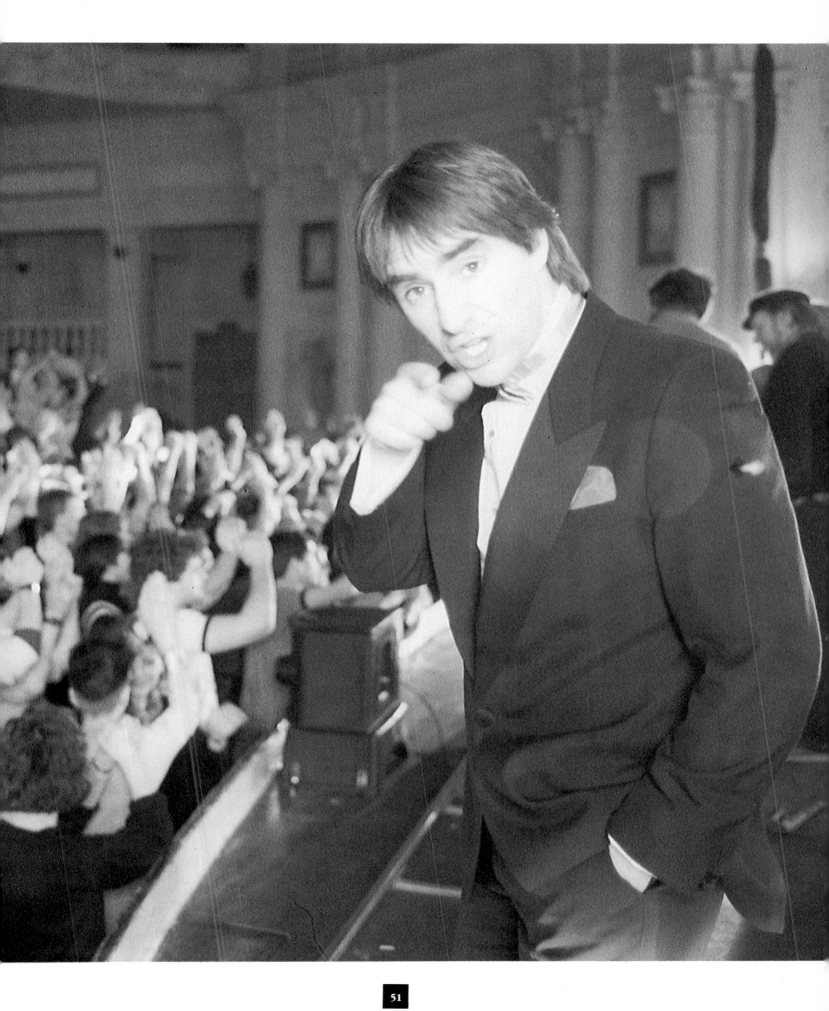

on, and I respected it, there were a lot of interesting things being done. But I don't think I ever saw it as a danger to my own career."

In fact, Chris had a number of other, far more pressing fears...fears which 'Crusader' did very little to alleviate. Where to turn next? Beyond consolidating his position in countries which had already welcomed his music, the album opened no new territories to him. A string of major open-air concerts in Canada, opening — once again! — for Supertramp, could only reinforce his feelings of stagnation. He felt he was offering his audience nothing new, that he was simply treading water. And, as if to make things even worse, his relationship with Dave Margereson, too, was on rocky ground.

"There were quite a few times when various people thought it was all over, not only between A&M and Chris, but between myself and Chris as well," admits Dave. "It felt very hard at times. We had virtually no record company funding to try and build a market with, and as each album went by the feeling was; well, *we* knew what made Chris so special, but other people obviously didn't... otherwise he'd be known in places other than Ireland and Canada."

Record sales and concert receipts in those particular areas convinced Dave that there were enough people out there to make further records and shows worthwhile, but this alone was insufficient for Chris' career to progress further. Like so many artists before him, Chris seemed to have found a comfortable cult niche,

where so many sales and seats were guaranteed, but there would never be any advancing. He simply wasn't reaching — or wasn't capable of reaching — the people whose support would elevate him to a higher status.

"We were plugging away on the live side because that was the only way we could get Chris heard," says Dave. "Radio wasn't interested in him for the usual reason of an artist not fitting in with their immediate requirements — in other words, he wasn't fashionable enough. So we toured and toured, and in so doing, I spent an awful lot of money, my own earnings, in funding the Chris de Burgh project. And there were times when I really felt like jacking it in, cutting my losses and simply getting out. I went up to Canada one time with the thought firmly in mind of it being the end of the line. I was getting enormously in debt and my business was suffering to the point where I thought I would have to shut it down. I really was thinking, 'That's it, I'll manage Supertramp and that'll be it.' But I got to the gig and it was just like he'd jumped out of that cupboard playing 'Hot Barrel Hannah' again. And I thought 'That's it, we've *got* to get this going again'."

Dave took his dilemma to Derek Green. "We had quite a blow up over where we were going with Chris," remembers Derek. "Dave showed me just how deep in the hole he was, how much of his own money had been put into Chris, and I was furious with him, as a friend, that he would put so much in. But I got my head of finance in to go over his accounts, then I went to Jerry Moss (the 'M' in A&M) and explained Dave's position, how he believed in Chris, how he was convinced that if only we persevered, one day everything that had been poured in would be repaid…as, indeed, it has been. Then Dave composed a letter to Jerry explaining much the same things, and Jerry, in his own generous way, agreed with the proposals."

In Dave's favour was Moss' awareness of how correct Dave's judgements had been in the past. Supertramp was now the best selling act in A&M's history, to the extent that when the company itself ran into financial difficulties towards the end of 1978 — a result of having overestimated one-time hotshot Peter Frampton's selling power — it was Supertramp alone who put the label back on its feet with their 'Breakfast In America' album. The shot in the arm that success gave the record company was like a whole new lease of life. Within a year, New Wave signings Joe Jackson, The Police and Squeeze had obliterated not only the very real corporate embarrassment precipitated by the Sex Pistols' debacle, but the shadow of extinction as well. And now, with Jerry Moss having agreed to alleviate at least some of Chris' outstanding debts and thus facilitate the recording of one more album, Chris himself rallied… and

straight away found himself with the biggest selling record of the year in Norway. And with the minimum of publicity as well.

"Norway has only four million inhabitants, and I always assumed a big seller over there meant something like 25,000, which is gold record status in Ireland," says Chris. "'Eastern Wind' ended up selling 125,000 copies — the only album to have done better than that is 'Abbey Road' by The Beatles. I was in the chart there for 18 months, 'Eastern Wind' was voted album of the year, I was voted artist of the year (a unique honour at a time when the assassinated John Lennon was topping polls everywhere else around the world). At one point I had five albums in the Norwegian chart all at the same time, with 'Eastern Wind' at number one. I just couldn't believe it, because it wasn't as if I was even

known out there — 'Crusader' had sold less than 12,000 copies in over a year!"

Chris couldn't help but reflect on one particular evening in Los Angeles two years previous. He and the band had been sitting round drinking, toasting each other and talking of their dreams. Unanimously, they began to plot out their ideal future...total world domination. Says Jeff Philips, "We knew then, we were going to make it."

"It was very strange," Dave Margereson reflects, "because the first time Chris played in Scandinavia he had a terrible time. He was playing in front of a room full of drunken students, all on their Friday night out; he was booed off stage basically... he refused to leave, of course, but he did cut his set short. So it's funny that he should then take off so enormously there. Maybe people admired his pluck, the way he kept going back there."

The success of 'Eastern Wind' convinced Dave once and for all that he was right to stay with Chris. "I knew that if it could happen in one place, then it would happen in others." He hoped, however, that when it did happen, it would be with a more representative album. Derek Green admits that he personally "loathed" 'Eastern Wind', that he would have been quite happy for Chris to have scrapped it and started again... and that was despite its success. "That album was corny, it was desperate, it was a lot of things," he alleges. "But it wasn't Chris."

Chris agrees. "The key thing about each album is that it's usually written right after about ten months of touring, so all the pressures and emotions I have inside come out in the writing. It's a release valve for me. People say 'Eastern Wind' is a very rock-orientated album, and it is. It was written on the back of about 130 shows, and it wasn't only my experience which went into it, but that of the band as well. 'Eastern Wind' was the first time I'd worked with them in the studio ('Crusader' was recorded with session men) so there were a lot of other influences going into it. That, possibly, is one reason why it came out like it did.

"The mistake I made, I think, was listening too much to what other people thought, without my actually agreeing with them. There are a couple of songs on there I wish I hadn't recorded, but which were included simply because other people liked them. Since then, I've only recorded with the band sporadically. I feel that recording requires a totally different discipline to live work, that studio technique is something that people learn over a number of years. And I think they would be the first to agree with me."

'Eastern Wind' was an almost schizophrenic collection, boasting as it did some of Chris' strongest work to date, and some of his weakest. In the first category there fell the title track, written about the situation in Iran at the time, "an observation of the whole sweeping of Eastern culture and a comment on how a man in the West felt threatened by it all."

'The Traveller', too, was a welcome addition to Chris' canon, its soaring, triumphant melody a sharp contrast to the aura of menace which oozed inexorably through the lyric. And a sharp contrast to the mock-reggae soup that was 'Record Company Bash', a song which Derek Green describes as, "Awful, awful and insulting. A lot of people who were literally knocking their brains out for Chris could have taken very personal offence at that song." At the same time, however, he admits Chris did have a very valid frustration... or at least, he thought he had.

The lurid scenario painted by the song, of

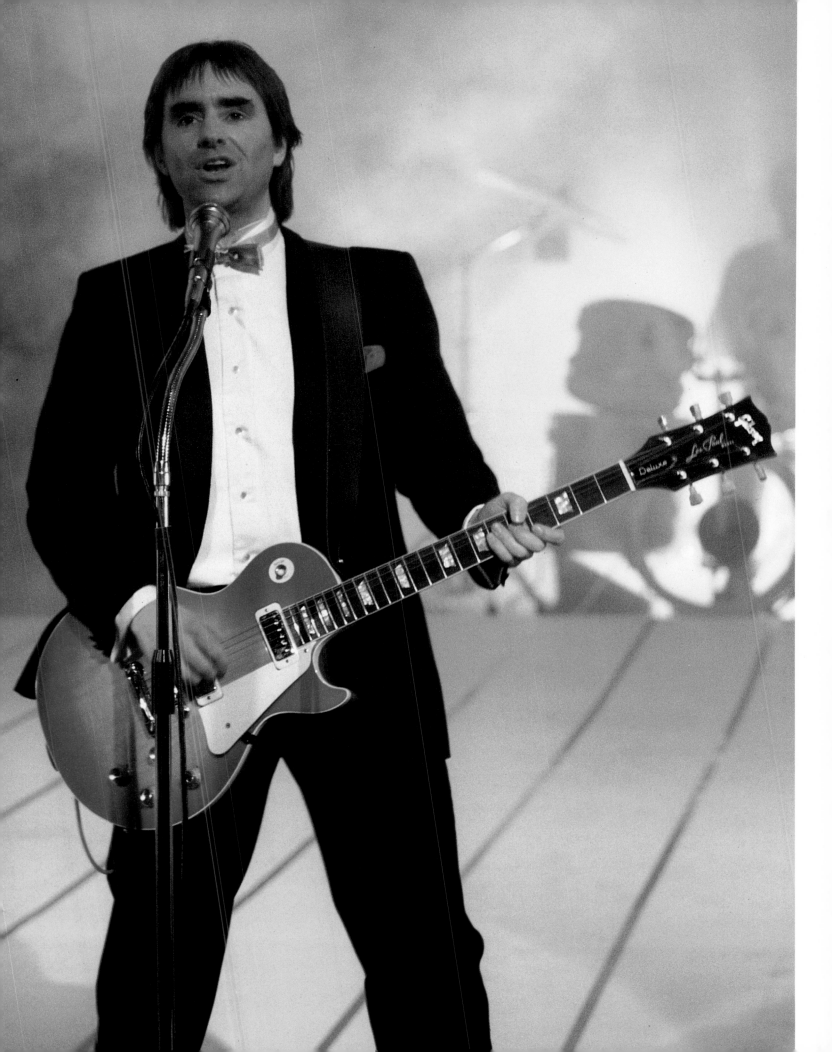

sex and drugs and women in wardrobes singing out-of-tune Beatles' songs, was merely camouflage for the very real sense of disillusion Chris was feeling. He was simply striking out at the most obvious target, record company excess, concentrating his anger in just one of the scores of different directions he could have channelled it. "That song wasn't directed at A&M," Chris says. "It was simply my observations on that curious phenomenon of record company executives who spend their time driving around in limos, or flying first class, and then complaining about the cost of recording and promoting their artists. It was just a general swipe, but it wasn't meant to be taken seriously."

There's a woman in the wardrobe singing Beatles out of tune
And a salesman in the corner trying to blow up a burst balloon
And the Managing Director, he's a lying on his back
He's got ice cream on his trousers and he's planning his attack
It's just another record company bash
Nice to know they've got the cash.

Jokiness apart, 'Record Company Bash' was a plea for moderation. Chris was certainly astute enough to know that the way into the market-place was not through the bladders of the press corps but through the hearts of the public: parties, receptions and the like were all very nice, but if money had to be spent on his career, Chris wanted it spent on those aspects of it which mattered, like keeping him on the road and in the studio. If people wanted to do obscene things with video machines, that was up to them. But Chris didn't want to end up paying for it.

"Chris has always been aware of exactly what's going on around him," says Kenny Thomson, "And he always wants to know. In terms of his day-to-day dealings, he's always been hard, wanting to know facts and figures, where the money's going, what we're doing in this place or that. He's always been aware."

With what he now describes as an ill-considered eye for the North American market, Chris recorded 'Eastern Wind' in Toronto, with American producer Dave Anderle. During the sixties, Anderle had been a leading light of CAFF, the Community Action for Fact and Freedom, which flourished with the first stirrings of Los Angeles hippydom — and that despite his having been responsible for giving Frank Zappa, the emergent scene's fiercest local detractor — his first major recording contract. A close friend of Brian Wilson during the making of The Beach Boys' legendary 'Smile' album, president of that same group's shortlived Brother label, Anderle made his name in the 1970s for producing a string of exquisite sounding albums for Rita Coolidge, Kris Kristofferson

Top: Chris with Al Marnie.
Above: Chris interviewing his own band on air at station OZFM, Newfoundland, 1980.

and the Ozark Mountain Daredevils —
credentials which must have sounded very safe
when his collaboration with Chris was first
mooted. As so often happens, however, any
expectations which may have been engendered
by his recent track record were quickly
evaporated...in 1981, when Anderle produced
the first album by California punk band, The
Circle Jerks, the rumour flew that they had
been alerted to his work by the cutting edge
which shone throughout 'Eastern Wind'.

The success of 'Eastern Wind' highlighted
the often perplexing paradox between artistic
and commercial glories; certainly Chris felt
somewhat disorientated when an album which
his closest allies hated should be the one which
125,000 complete strangers took to their
hearts. In his own mind, he wanted to return
to values which had somehow been lost in the
scramble for that sort of acceptance, a return to
the fiery passion of 'Spanish Train', coupled
with the naive tenderness of 'Castle Walls' and
'Perfect Day'. But the fear was always the
same. Would people want that kind of thing?
Might not such a move simply send him
hurtling back into the abyss, a cult artist
whose every future action was dependent on
how many fingers it took to count up the
supporters of the last one? The answer was
elusive. It was also simple.

Top: The Band in Rheinterassen, Bonn, 1977.

with the songs which I considered said the most about my music.

"Really, that was the best thing I could ever have done, release that album. So many people would see it and say 'Oh, *he* did that, I heard it on the radio...' It introduced so many new people to my music. It was certainly my ticket in Europe, it really banged me up there. It was Top Five in Germany, it did almost as well everywhere else. And I followed it with such renewed excitement and inspiration. I was feeling much more solid and sure of myself, mainly because I knew that people were interested. If you have the feeling that no-one out there is interested, you don't really give it all you've got, but I knew now that people were, in West Germany and Norway and all these other places."

Germany is a country which has remained particularly close to Chris' heart. "The first time I was there was in 1977, with Supertramp. We were playing arenas, and I got a great response. Nothing really happened there for about three years, and then I started doing television shows out there. It grew very quickly — suddenly I was being rung up to be asked if I could make it over to Munich or somewhere to replace somebody else on a show, they'd dropped out or whatever. And I would always say yes, of course I could. Then we did a small tour, around the time of 'Eastern Wind', four dates which started with a Bierkeller in Bonn. It was a beautiful day — before the show we were sitting outside drinking beer, and watching the river boats go by, and I just thought it was such a wonderful country, and really hoped things would take off for me there, simply so I could go back. The scenery was so beautiful, the people were all so friendly — there were only 40 or 50 people at the show, but the response was so warm." Chris returned to Germany in support of the 'Best Moves' album, riding this time on the crest of a wave of popular support which, he admits, still leaves him lost for words.

'Best Moves' was a compilation album aimed straight at the commercial heart of Christmas 1981, and looking back, Chris admits, "To be honest, I hadn't known what I was going to do before 'Best Moves' came along. I'd never thought about releasing a compilation. It was the Canadian record company who actually suggested it. Although I had never had a hit single there (and wasn't going to, until 1986 saw 'The Lady In Red' top the chart for over three months), my album sales, and ticket sales were enormous. So they phoned and said they wanted to have something out for the Christmas market and why didn't I put together a compilation. So I recorded a few new songs, and put them in

A lot of water has gone under the bridge since Chris compiled 'Best Moves'; a new convert today would doubtless find it lacking in a myriad of ways. As a summary of his career up to that point, however, 'Best Moves' could scarcely have been better executed. Two new songs, 'Waiting For The Hurricane' and 'Every Drop Of Rain', together with a live version of 'Broken Wings' taken from a live album released in South Africa only, two years previous, were joined by a selection of more familiar material whose only real failing was the omission of 'Turning Round'. 'Best Moves' might have been conceived simply as a stop-gap, a means of keeping Chris' name alive in the territories where he did matter, but very quickly it took on a whole new life of its own. Its impact in Europe was quite astounding. "Germany went wild for it," Dave Margereson proudly boasts. "Switzerland, Sweden,

everywhere. In England it didn't do quite so well immediately (it peaked at number 65), but over a period of time, it has outsold pretty much everything else released around the same time. That is Chris' greatest strength, not only in England but all over the world. Most artists' records have a fairly short life, a few months, maybe a year if they're lucky. Chris is one of the very few whose records continue to sell in fairly large quantities over many years. 'Spanish Train', a decade after it was released, is still selling phenomenally well all over the place (the album finally went platinum in Britain in 1986)."

Chris himself was amazed to hear that 'Best Moves' has even been used as a teaching aid, his use of the English language and his clear enunciation lending themselves perfectly to English classes. And not only in Europe… "A friend came back from a trip to China and

said, 'Oh yeah, you're on the curriculum out there.' So much for literary education! But it's a great compliment, knowing that there are people walking around whose knowledge of the English language comes from listening to my songs!"

Teaching aids aside, Chris admits it is curious that some two thirds of his worldwide sales come from countries where English is not spoken — France, Germany, Italy, Greece, even Russia. "I think my lyrics do make sense. It comes from the firm belief that if I spend a long time writing a lyric, it's because I really want them to be heard. And understood. We included French and German translations in some of the albums, just so people could get some idea of what it's all about, but at the same time, I used to wonder why I bothered writing lyrics. It is, in fact, very much a testament to the artist, that he is expressing such universal emotion in his music. But at the same time, there is a completely new breed of European who is determined to learn English. They listen to the radio, they listen to the

World Service, they buy records like mine and Leonard Cohen's and Bob Dylan's and they teach themselves English."

Chris toured Europe in the wake of 'Best Moves', renewed vigour apparent in every move he made. He was planning a new album already, and in a move which was to split his allies into separate camps almost as clearly defined as had 'Eastern Wind', he called synthesizer whizzkid — and fellow Mismanagement artiste — Rupert Hine in to produce it. "The first person we thought of was Glyn Johns, who handled the recording of 'Every Drop Of Rain' and 'Waiting For The Hurricane', but he wasn't keen. I'd written six or seven new songs by that time, so next we invited Gus Dudgeon (of Elton John, and David Bowie's 'Space Oddity' fame) to come over to Dusseldorf to see a show. I had a few demos which I'd done in an hotel room in Paris — they weren't very good, and I told him that I wasn't particularly happy with all the stuff, although the seeds of a new album were there. Unfortunately, he didn't like any of the songs, and wrote back to say he wasn't interested. I must be honest and say I thought he was very wrong, not because I thought the songs were particularly good, but because I knew there was better things to come."

The tour ended in March, and Chris immediately turned his attention full time to the problem of the new album. "I was trying to build a show around the new songs, looking at the dynamics in exactly the same way as I would make an album. I don't view either as a simple random collection of songs, thrown together in any order; I always write for the key points, the first and last tracks on each side, which means, dynamically, that the last song on the album has to be the big one, the statement. Track one, side one, also has to come in with a punch — on a scale of ten, the opener should be a nine, the closing song a ten. I hadn't got those songs when I played the tape to Gus, but now I was thinking seriously about it, and things were moving along. I was headlining huge places in Canada, in Norway, I knew I had to give the audience songs with that little extra power. So, through April and May I was writing continually, and by the beginning of the summer, I had virtually the whole album in place.

"The problem with being a solo writer, is that I like to have somebody I can bounce my ideas off — if I know who the producer is, say, then I can zero in on him, almost as if I'm writing for his capabilities rather than my own. So the songs I wrote and played to Gus, I'd had no-one in mind, there wasn't anybody for me to aim the songs at. But by the time I started writing seriously, Rupert Hine had introduced himself. He contacted Kenny Thomson and said, quite simply, that I had always been undersold on record — he saw the strengths of the live performance, and he knew

65

the records, and he just thought there was a yawning gap. His thing was to try and create what he heard in live terms, but to do it in the studio. I was thrilled, because I had admired his first album tremendously."

One of the 1980s' most interesting discoveries, Rupert Hine first hit the public eye during the early seventies when he was discovered by Deep Purple bassist Roger Glover, and signed to Purple's own in-house label, Purple Records. Throughout the 1970s, he worked with a variety of different acts, ranging from the beautifully sublime — Kevin Ayers' superlative 'Confessions Of Dr. Dream' album — to the ridiculous; Quantum Jump, and their 'Lone Ranger' novelty hit. The Ayers album apart, however, it was not until 1981, when his own 'Immunity' album was released, that Rupert achieved serious acknowledgement. Very quickly he earned himself a reputation as a man with an ear for the all too precious American market, another consideration which was not lost on Chris, even if his closest associates still weren't overjoyed at the prospect.

"Working with Rupert was a marriage which initially seemed dangerous. I know Derek Green thought it was a dreadful idea initially, but the more people said that, the more excited about the whole thing I became. I could easily have made another safe record,

got in a producer who sounded like he could come up with some really smooth, slick production that would have suited me, got together with him and made exactly the same kind of record we always knew we would. But I don't want to do things like that, I don't want to 'grow old' with my audience, and I certainly don't want to trot out the same tired old clichés every time I make a new record. By putting myself with a few different producers, the difference in style is dramatic, it keeps me fresh, and I think it keeps my fans fresh. Rupert really is one of the most creative producers around, to the point where it sometimes gets very frustrating because he's spending hours and hours trying to get just one piano 'plink'. But it's worth it in the end."

"What Rupert has done for me is fill the gaps," Chris said at the time. "I'm painfully aware of what my shortcomings are in the studio. I'm like the architect who draws up the plan, but I'm not really very good at assembling the bricks and building the basic foundation. That's where Rupert comes in. Then, when the building is half up, I come back in again and start working on the decoration, the wallpaper and so on. That's the way I can describe it best. So he filled my shortcomings in the studio, and on the things he's not that interested in, like the vocals, I just go to town."

CHAPTER NINE

*P*SYCHE WAS NOW *satisfied that her destruction was at hand, being obliged to go with her own feet directly down to Erebus, the God of Darkness. Wherefore, to make no delay of what was not to be avoided, she went to the top of a high tower to precipitate herself headlong, thus to descend the shortest way to the Shades below. But a voice from the tower said, "Why, poor, unlucky girl, dost thou design to put an end to thy days in so dreadful a manner? And what cowardice makes thee sink under this last danger who hast been so miraculously supported in all thy former?" Then the voice told her how by a certain cave she might reach the realms of Pluto, and how to avoid all the dangers of the road, to pass by Cerberus, the three headed dog, and prevail on Charon, the ferryman, to take her across the black River Styx to Hades, and to bring her back again.*

CHRIS DE BURGH -THE VIDEO

INCLUDES: DON'T PAY THE FERRYMAN ● SPANISH TRAIN ● THE TRAVELLER ● A SPACEMAN CAME TRAVELLING ● PATRICIA THE STRIPPER

"I remember when I was writing for 'The Getaway', I'd spent a little time with Rupert — he'd come over to Dublin and listened to what I had so far, that kind of thing. And I looked at the running order of the album, and I thought it really lacked a powerful song, an exciting part. I was playing my guitar, getting to that emotional point where the subconscious leaks out and I got the line...'Don't pay the ferryman'. And when I got it I went, 'I love it, what is it?' It's at that point that I have to bring all my influences to bear, literary, historical, whatever, and I figured out the Ferryman was definitely Charon. I had this image, and I took it from there, trying out different ideas and themes. The spoken words are from Shakespeare, *The Tempest*, when the boatman is describing the storm and saying *'We were dead of sleep and all clapped under hatches'*. I really thought that was appropriate. And one poem that I've always loved is *Childe Roland To The Dark Tower Came*, by Robert Browning, particularly the point where he feels it's his destiny to go to this place, he doesn't know why, but he is driven to it. And he suddenly recognises it..."

Burningly it came on me all at once
This was the place! Those two hills on the right
Crouched like two bulls locked horn in horn in fight
While to the left, a tall scalped mountain...

"And the idea of this guy thundering through the night and suddenly realising 'My God, this is it, this is the place', just hit me. 'There's the tower and there's the boat.' And he knows he's got to go on, although it may cost him his life.

"All around him there are noises and shapes, all these things that have been sent to scare him into paying the boatman; the dancing skeletons on the water, the thunder and the lightning. It's very vivid for me, a sort of mist, all in shadows. And still the boatman says, 'Pay me now,' and he says, 'No.' And the voice comes from the other side, 'Don't do it'. And at last he gets there, at last he's across the river..."

Dauntless the slug horn to my lips I set
And blew. "Childe Roland to the Dark Tower came."

"There's no moral to the song, it's not 'Don't pay till you get over to the other side'. It's supposed to be primarily theatre in music. It's just a bit of excitement. I love from time to time to set up a tune where it's so breathless that you don't know what's happened until it's finished. I enjoyed making that record a lot."

The single of 'Ferryman' was accompanied by a video, and very quickly the wisdom of the move became apparent, the MTV channel latching on to it to such a degree that it became one of the most played videos of the entire year in the United States. And that despite Chris' reservations on the subject. "I'm terribly cynical about videos; people had hits before them, and quite honestly, it's at the stage now where I think a bad video can hinder a song, and while it's still possible to have a hit simply because of the video, I don't think it can make a hit artist. And there's a big difference.

"My attitude towards my own videos is that if they want to do one, they can get as much footage of anything they like, but I will do nothing more than mime to the song. Then they can splice it all together, make a collage. But I will never act in a video, because I think it looks corny (the collage effect had already been used to great effect on Chris' first video, three years before the medium finally exploded into the open, illustrating the title track of the 'Crusader' album).

"I remember reading a review where a member of another band said that he came up

The 'I Love The Night' video.

with the wonderful idea of writing a song and thinking of a video concept at the same time. I laughed, because I have been doing that ever since my first album. I discovered that the easiest way to write was to visualise everything first. Especially on my second album, where every song was a story or a series of pictures and images."

'The Getaway' was completed by July 1982, and, says Chris, "The record just picked me up and threw me in a direction that I knew I needed to go in. It was so fresh, you could just feel it jumping out of the songs. I felt that record contained some of my best writing since the 'Spanish Train' record. The motivation for it was so strong, partly because the compilation had done so well, partly because I'd had such a terrific year emotionally. I played 120 shows across the world and to have done that, and to have sold out virtually every one, whilst feeling so good was terrific."

It was that feeling of optimism which dominated 'The Getaway', both musically and in terms of its reception. A number one across Europe and in Australia, clocking up *en route* sales of 800,000 in Germany, and attaining double platinum status in Switzerland, the album also saw Chris making some inroads into the American market. And, almost hilariously, the power of Chris' performance, the mystical feel to both lyrics and production, saw him fleetingly bracketed with, or even mistaken for, Blue Oyster Cult, with whose own 'Don't Fear The Reaper' Chris' single earned several favourable comparisons.

'Don't Pay The Ferryman' had regular plays on the album orientated FM networks, so regular that at one point it crossed over to the Top 40 AM stations and for a short time became the most played record on American radio — an achievement for which Charlie Prevost takes full credit. "I'd relocated in the U.S. after the 1977 tour, and was trying to break the 'Crusader' album over there, but it was just impossible to get the American market to wake up to Chris de Burgh, he simply didn't fit. Then when 'Ferryman' came out, I was very much involved in promoting that in America, although I think too much water had gone under the bridge between Chris and I for me to really pull out all the stops. But I pushed that song, and when it charted, I really believe I can take all the credit for that."

The song finally peaked at number 34 on the US chart (14 places higher than its British best). "And when I toured there the following year, the reaction was fantastic. I really didn't expect anything like it, even though 'Ferryman' had done so well. Although I had done a lot of work in America, touring and promoting, I kept remembering our last trip, when we went from playing to however many thousands of people across the border in Canada, then slipped across the border and didn't see anybody! It was all 'Who is this Crystal Bird?' and 'Christopher, that Burgie fellow'."

Kenny Thomson remembers arriving at one venue to find Chris actually billed as Crystal Bird! "It got to the stage where I was introducing him as C de B, only for people to confuse him with the Charlie Daniels Band!"

"No-one knew who I was, yet in a way, that was a good thing because it does help you keep your head nice and small," says Chris. "It encourages you to go out there and *work*, and to establish yourself as a performing artist."

In actual fact, there was a handful of areas where Chris was guaranteed a good turn-out. In the North-East, his Canadian fame preceded him to the extent where local radio stations picked up on the sounds of their contemporaries across the border, and fans arrived knowing his songs quite as well as anybody north of the Great Lakes. More surprisingly, Texas also accepted him very early on, as Chris discovered when he toured the state with Peter Frampton in 1979. Four years had passed since Frampton was the Star To End All Stars in the annals of American pop mythology, four years in which his career had taken a thorough battering on the back of just one ill-conceived LP and a disastrous move into the film world via Robert Stigwood's appalling celluloid production of *Sergeant Pepper's Lonely Hearts Club Band*. A forgotten hero and an unknown Irishman — it was hardly the most alluring of bills, but in the Lone Star state, Chris was greeted with capacity crowds at every show, and was even persuaded to give up some of his free time to headline smaller gigs in his own right (several years later, Chris repaid Frampton for all his assistance on that tour, by inviting him to join him on the bill of a Dublin festival).

"The first radio station in America to play Chris seriously was a Heavy Metal grunge station in Texas," says Kenny. "They were playing 'Don't Pay The Ferryman', then from there it got to the state where they'd play Def Leppard, then one of Chris' *ballads*, then something by Iron Maiden. We knew he always had the ability to transcend musical cultures, but even we didn't think it could go *that* far!

"I found in America that, although people might not be familiar with Chris' name, there was a lot of song recognition. If you said he was the guy who did 'Don't Pay The Ferryman' or 'Spaceman Came Travelling', they immediately knew what you were talking about. And I found a similar thing with journalists; mention Chris and they would immediately think 'Oh yes, the folk singer, the story teller, the guy who's big in Brazil'. (Later, of course, he was to be pigeon-holed once again, this time on the strength of 'The Lady In Red'.) When you see him live, he's as dynamic as anybody, but the media —

Top: Chris with Heidi Bigge of A&M Germany.
Above: Kenny Thompson, Jurgen Larson, Chris and Dave Margerson.

particularly in Britain — refused to cross that line. There was an enormous mental block, and the great thing is, he was successful despite that. People knew about him without having to read his name in the music papers. They knew when he had records out, they knew when he'd be touring — I don't know how the word got about, but I had people writing and phoning the office wanting to know about gigs before I'd even confirmed them. For the 1986 tour, we put two adverts in the press, one in *The Times*, the other in the London *Standard*. And eight British shows sold out immediately... and that was three months before the tour opened."

For his latest American tour, Chris was to spend a month touring with MOR supergroup Asia, a mismatch he was to resent for some time to come. "A bunch of 'Star' idiots," is how he described the band later. "I spent one month on the road with them and although they were obviously a bigger act than me in America, I'd outsell them ten to one in

Europe... and they didn't even have the good grace to say hello to me. I'm not bitter, I just thought it was pretty disgusting."

"Steve Howe and John Wetton were the only members of the band to even say hello to us throughout the tour," says Kenny Thomson.

Asia had just released their second album, the follow-up to an enormously successful début set, which seemed destined to ensure their top flight success for years to come. Unfortunately, things weren't going as planned. Reviews were disparaging, sales disappointing. The tour, set up months before the release of the LP, swiftly developed into a fiasco when the original 36 date itinerary was pruned down to 25. Seventeen thousand seat venues were often scarcely one-eighth full; on more than one occasion, the band's manager would ask Kenny Thomson if he'd take less money than had been agreed, simply so Asia could break even on the evening's expenses. The strain was showing on the band, too. Says Kenny, "They were on the verge of breaking up, forces within the line-up were pulling it apart, and they treated us all like shit... and that despite his selling half the tickets for the shows in Texas."

More successful were the dates Chris played with Eddie Money. Remembers Kenny: "He asked Chris to go along to some radio interviews with him, usually in places where there was no acceptance for Chris, where he was completely unknown. And at the station he'd demand the DJ played Chris' latest album. An absolute gentleman. Asia simply didn't want to know..."

Life on the road for Chris and the band, understandably, was not slow to take on a reality all of its own; however, whereas some bands prefer to subordinate their private existences with Bacchanalian revelry, Chris gleefully admits that he utilises most of his free time to dream up practical jokes with which to keep the rest of the band on their toes. Having

exhausted the possibilities inherent in ordering breakfasts for everybody at six in the morning, which he happily admits is a truly dreadful thing to do to anyone, he now devotes himself to setting the rest of the band up for any number of repercussions, whilst maintaining a discreet distance from the proceedings himself. "We have an enormous amount of fun on the road. With six very different personalities around, I never laugh as much as I do when we're all together".

One evening, the band found themselves sharing a hotel in Britain with a business conference — whose managing director was quite unwisely placed in the room between Chris and Jeff Phillips.

Chris' first move was to warn Jeff that Glen Morrow was on his way up with a bucket of water. He would knock twice, then when Jeff opened up...splash. He then rang Glen, saying Jeff was expecting a visitor, and that it' would be a great opportunity to throw a bucket of water at him. "I told him, 'All you have to do is walk up there, knock twice, and you'll get him.' Then I just stood by my door, and watched as the whole scene developed, exactly as I'd planned. Glen goes up, knocks on the door. His bucket of water goes in, another bucket flies out, they're both drenched. That was it, World War Three, and I just spent the next four hours in fits. Jeff went completely crazy... he thought I was in the next room, and he spent two hours banging a stool against the wall. And of course, it didn't bother me, because I had the managing director as insulation. And the next morning, we went downstairs and the manageress came up to me and said, I'm afraid you're going to have to leave. So I said, Why? What's happened, what's going on? Well, she said, there were terrible things going on all night. I, of course, didn't know a thing about it. I never heard a thing!"

•   •   •

Top: 'Mrs' Al Marnie.
Above: Oslo Airport, 1980, waiting on yet another plane.
Right: Chris, re-signing with Rondor Music, in January 1986. Left to right: Dave Margereson, Stuart Hornall (Rondor), Chris and Kenny Thompson.

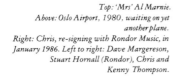

'The Getaway' gave Chris only his second ever British album chart entry. In taking three months to reach the Top 30, however, it proved something of a disappointment to the people around him (it has since gone gold in the UK). "I thought we were really going to crack it with that one," says Dave Margereson. "The way the music was presented on that album was a real turning point for Chris. Up to that point it was great songs, a great voice, but somehow we still didn't seem to be grabbing the Progressive ear. Chris still had something of a folkie image in England, something which went back to his one man and his guitar period, the all-round nice guy with his nice songs. But Rupert Hine did a magnificent job and we ended up with an album you can play anywhere, anytime, and one which will hold its own against any of the more accepted Progressive albums.

"Up to that point I think Chris' albums were almost an acquired taste: the romantics liked them, women liked them because they could see Chris was sensitive... that's a hopeless generalisation really, but he did have that kind of image. 'The Getaway' broke away from all that. But while it became his most instantly successful record yet, it still couldn't break him away from that image."

Chris toured the world in support of 'The Getaway', a mammoth outing which sold out within days of being announced. But despite the obvious optimism such a reception instilled within him, there were worries as well. "I was convinced that it was going to be very difficult writing songs for the next album. I would be coming off the road in America in

September, and I had to have everything ready to take over to London in January. I hate that sort of pressure, because I think it makes it harder artistically if you know you have to have something done by a certain time. I had to be very disciplined and chain myself to a desk and tape record everything for six hours a day. And for the first three or four weeks, nothing happened. It was the most incredibly frustrating thing. But the more frustrated I got, the more I realised the greater the chance of getting a song out.

"After banging on the table and ranting and raving, I relax into a mental condition where a few words come into my mind and then the rest of it is like a puzzle you try to work out. It's an incredible game of trying to seduce those ideas out. Finally I got 10, 12 songs together, which I brought over to Rupert in London and we played through them and both sensed that six of them were very, very good. But while the other four would have worked perfectly on 'The Getaway', they just wouldn't have cracked it on this one. We knew we'd have to pull something very special out of the bag this time. So I actually wrote four more songs in the studio, something which I'd never done before and, to be honest, I'd never want to do again."

'High On Emotion' was one such song. "I had the melody line and the chorus worked out over Christmas, and I liked it but I wasn't sure where to take it from there. I remember sitting at the piano with Rupert, just going over and over what I had, going through every permutation and suddenly the whole song just came out, like I had somehow released a

Above: Jeff, Marcel Avram of Mama Concerts, Chris and Ian Kojima.
Below: Jeff as the Statue of Liberty.

blocked pipe. It really was that kind of rush, everything — the words, the chords, BANG. And I turned to Rupert and said, 'If I never work with you again, I want to remember this moment as probably the peak of my artistic creativity.' It was immensely exciting."

'Man On The Line', the new album, was a far darker collection than its predecessor. "With 'The Getaway', Rupert was an unknown, as far as production work went. Then he did my album, Saga's 'Heads Or Tails'and The Fixx album, 'The Shuttered Room', and suddenly he realised he really had to prove himself with his subsequent work. And I think he was prepared to accept less involvement in the music than he had in the past, because he was so anxious to establish himself as a producer. He wanted to make an album which stood up alongside everything else he'd done in 1983 as an example of his own talents, which wasn't a bad thing by any means, but I don't think anybody would say 'Man On The Line' is my best album, although

there is a lot of stuff on there which I think is really good. 'High On Emotion' is one which I particularly like, 'Transmission Ends' I absolutely adore, and 'Much More Than This'.

"But it was a spotty kind of a record. I think things like 'Sound Of A Gun' (which featured a guest vocal from a passing Tina Turner),and 'I Love The Night' could have been slightly differently done. They sounded angry, which they weren't meant to. But it's impossible for a writer to keep turning out extraordinary albums, you have to tread water a little, then make certain you come out with something special the next time. Either that, or do nothing for however many years… But I'm a working artist, I love to perform, therefore I've got to put something out to justify my next tour. As long as I believe in what I'm doing, I'm happy for people to hear it. But I certainly don't expect my fans to like everything I do."

●   ●   ●

On April 17, 1984, Chris' first daughter, Rosanna Diane, was born. It was an event Chris and Diane had almost given up hoping for. Two years previously, while Chris was away working on 'The Getaway', Diane almost died after the most serious of several miscarriages she was to suffer. "Diane was alone in the house, and she collapsed with an ectopic pregnancy; she hadn't even known she was pregnant. Thankfully, a doctor, a friend of ours, just happened to be passing the house and decided to drop by to visit. He rushed Diane to hospital... another half an hour and I'd have lost her. When Rosanna was born, I went out and bought the two biggest bottles of champagne I could find, one for the doctor, and one for the surgeon at the hospital, with the message 'Thank you for the gift of life'."

Rosanna was born with none of the complications which attended Diane's earlier pregnancy. Her birth, Chris said later, "meant more to me than any pop success. My family definitely comes first, the music business second. I would jack everything in tomorrow if I thought my work was affecting my family. If Diane said she wasn't going to go on tour with me any more (she now accompanies him on nearly every tour, and they are never separated for more than a week), then I would stop."

So strong were his feelings on the subject that, at just 10 weeks old, Rosanna was on the road with Chris, touring Canada for three and a half weeks in her pushchair. "Rosanna was born during that period after the recording of the album, but before I went out on tour, and I was absolutely besotted. We were so lucky to have a child that I wasn't going to risk anything. The idea of leaving her behind while I spent four weeks in America, and did 60 dates across Europe simply didn't enter my mind."

"Chris always takes his family out with him," Kenny Thomson says. "I don't think he'd do it if he couldn't, if he didn't have that stabilising force behind him. He would just flatly refuse. So we take the family, and we have a babysitter, and we try to gear the tours so we're not rushing around to a different place every day, we have reasonable gaps in the schedule so there isn't too much unrest and disturbance."

Throughout the summer, Chris concentrated his activities on open-air festivals in Europe and the United Kingdom, with a supporting cast that included REO Speedwagon, The Alarm, Men At Work and something approaching a quarter of a million fans. He toured with much the same show as the previous year — a stage festooned in telephone wires, and a set which drew predominantly from the most recent LPs. The biggest of all the shows was at the Nurnburgring in Germany where, after supporting sets by Rick Springfield, U2 and Joe Cocker, Chris played to over 100,000 fans.

Rosanna, on tour, 1985.

Yet when he headlined London's Crystal Palace
Bowl, the week after playing Liverpool's
International Festival Gardens, *New Musical
Express* described the show as "perhaps the
most prestigious he has ever played." The
irony was not lost on Chris... but any accolade,
however misinformed, was welcome in a land
where the popular music papers refused even to
acknowledge his existence, still clinging as
they were to the decade old vision of a little
guy strumming an acoustic guitar and singing
about windy nights, lonely skies and strippers
named Patricia.

"I couldn't just strum my guitar in front
of however many thousands of people after
bands like that had been on," Chris said after
the Nurnburgring show. "This isn't a one
man, one guitar folk thing, this is a major rock
'n' roll production."

That, in fact, was one of the prime
criticisms which Chris was to face when he took
the show on the road in the United Kingdom.
It was a production, a theatrical spectacular,
the slick outpourings of a well-oiled machine.
Nothing was left to chance. And at a time
when more and more pop idols were arriving
already couched in the neatly sanitised pre-
packaging of supermarket culture, Chris
admitted there was a certain amount of truth
in the accusation. "There is a school of thought
which says that when a band reaches a certain
point, they might as well not bother touring,
they could simply send out a film of
themselves, for all the audience contact their
show engenders. And during the 'Man On The
Line' tour, I knew I was getting very close to
that stage. We played the Nurnburgring, in
front of 100,000 people, and I thought,
'That's it, I've gone over the edge'.

"So one of the things I did was contact a
German TV guy, and we made a 45 minute
special which was just me at home, talking
about myself, which went out on German TV.
The record was doing well, but that show was
the killer, because I think people finally
realised that I was sincere about attempting to
cross that bridge again. And on the next tour,
for 'Into The Light', I made up my mind to
communicate more with the audience, to chat
between numbers and not simply trot out the
same old one-liners night after night. And I
think it worked; I was certainly happier with
that tour than any other.

"As far as going back to playing sweaty
little shows, though, gigging in front of 40
people in the *Rheinterassen* Bierkeller, which is
where we began the first German tour, that is
simply impossible today. The demand for
tickets is so great that we have to play the
largest venues possible, otherwise I could
spend the rest of the year simply playing one
city!"

He had already hammered that point
home the previous year, when he headlined
three shows at the massive Wembley Arena in
north-west London, and was then forced to

tack on a further two nights at the Hammersmith Odeon at the end of the tour to cope with the ticket demand. All five shows were sold out months in advance. And, almost predictably, the 'Man On The Line' tour saw Chris setting — or breaking — even more records. In Germany, for instance, he sold more concert tickets than any other artist, visiting or native. Merchandising alone brought in some £180,000 as the tour wound its way around the world.

Perhaps the most emotive of the summer shows was in Basle. "We were about to play 'Borderline', and I asked the audience to light me a fire for peace. There must have been 20,000 lights flickering in the darkness. It was like looking at the Milky Way."

Having admitted that 'Man On The Line'... "got a little too electronic for my taste, at least in parts," Chris was adamant from the start that its successor, on which he began work in the autumn of 1985, would be "much more natural. If a song demands a piano, I'll put a piano on it, or acoustic guitar or anything normal. It just struck me that the synthesizer was simply killing emotions stone dead. People were sick to death of hearing straight synthesizer, just like they got sick of seeing digital watches. All of a sudden people wanted to see a real watch again. That kind of thing. And there has been a general turning away from straight synthesizer music, more people moving back towards 'the real thing'.

"What I like to do, because I travel so much, is try and get an international reading, a general universal emotion. And right now I think I'm reading something approaching blind terror on a global scale. I don't think that people want innovation, they want comfort. 'Man On The Line' did better than any of my albums beforehand (honours conferred on the set included Chris' second successive award from the Maxell tape company, for the best LP recorded on that particular brand of tape), but even while I was still recording 'Into the Light' I knew it would do even better."

Early on in the sessions for the set, he promised, "The next record will be much more open and classical, as well as modern. A combination between 'The Getaway' and 'Spanish Train', but moved forward a couple of years, something which sounds exciting off the record and makes you want to go and catch the act live." He hinted at capturing "a Bruce Springsteen sound", if only to reflect the power of his live show, but when the time came, the plan was dropped, mercifully for the fans who had already had all they could take of Bruce during the unprecedented overkill of the previous 12 months.

The album's eventual opening cut, 'Last Night', had indeed been conceived as an epic showstopper of sorts, and was performed as such on the 1985 summer tour. "But I got a little bored with all those wailing saxophones," Chris admitted. "It seemed such an obvious way of doing the song, and one thing I found with the album was that if we recorded it in the obvious way, after a while it simply lost its sparkle. I think I re-recorded every single song on the set at least once..."

As a stop-gap between albums, a second compilation, 'The Very Best Of Chris de Burgh' was released by the Telstar label. The album had nothing to do with Chris — he was not consulted on either the songs included or

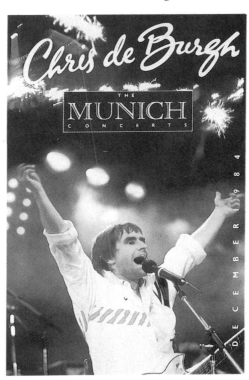

the running order. It was, quite simply, an arrangement between Mismanagement, A&M and Telstar, and was released only in the United Kingdom — much to the chagrin of Chris' other fans. The compilation was one of two possible releases; the other was a live album taken from Chris' Munich shows in 1984. A video of the concert was already available, however, and the feeling was that it would be somewhat presumptuous to expect people to buy both a video and an LP of the same show — which wasn't much help to fans without video machines! In the event, 'The Very Best Of...' undoubtedly achieved far more for Chris in the UK than a live album ever would have. It was an immediate hit, peaking at number six, and, thanks to a very heavy TV advertising campaign, the album finally brought home to people just how phenomenally successful Chris was threatening to be.

And so the build up to 'Into The Light' continued. All concerned were convinced it was going to be a monster. How big a monster, however, they could never have guessed.

Opposite, above: In Basle, Switzerland, before an audience of 35,000.
Opposite, below: Crystal Palace, London, 1985.

CHAPTER TEN

CHRIS DE BURGH
INTO THE LIGHT

'INTO THE LIGHT' was recorded in England, first at the Manor Studios in Oxfordshire (a poignant choice: the studios had come almost as far in the years since Mike Oldfield recorded 'Tubular Bells' there as Chris had in the years since he supported the film of the recording), then at Marcus Studio, in West London. Jeff Phillips and Glen Morrow, together with the rest of Chris' live band, bassist Al Marnie, saxophonist Ian Kojima and guitarist Danny McBride (who had replaced Tim Wynveen in the line-up after four years) and producer Paul Hardiman, joined him, as did a number of session men who were introduced to the sessions to stretch Chris in less familiar directions… and vice versa.

He wanted, he says, to capture the feel of the live show, to which end he brought his own band in on a lot of the tracks. Years of working together, years of mutual respect and support, had honed them into as precise a gauge of Chris' own needs as he could have wished for; indeed, it is the teamwork within the unit which is responsible for the often magical coherence of the live performance. It was this magic which Chris needed to capture on vinyl. And for the first time since 'Spanish Train & Other Stories', when the divide between his stage and studio solo personas was so successfully bridged, he succeeded.

"Everybody was pushed to be more creative than they have been on other people's records," says Chris with just a hint of pride. "Unfortunately, some of the outside musicians we tried out simply weren't up to it. However much they were interested in the project, they weren't interested enough. It was quite clear that their hearts weren't into it, and it wound up that we found most of them wanting. They had never, I don't think, worked with anybody as insistent on the mood coming off the music as I am… we had a couple of players down who were just so bad…and these guys were charging £400 a day! They were dreadful! Eventually we ended up with the nucleus you can hear on the album."

"Chris is the stubbornest man you could ever want to meet, although he'll always listen to, and consider, the other point of view," says Jeff Phillips. "In the studio, he knows exactly what he wants and he won't let anybody get away with trying to change things. A lot of times, I get carried off in the direction of good old rock 'n' roll, but he quickly puts a stop to it! He knows what he wants, and very often he'll write out a storyboard for the song, where it's going and what it means. Which is great… it's very rare you get to work with somebody and actually know what they're singing about!"

"When I write, I have a rhetorical debate with myself on paper; who's doing what in the song, what's the situation, what am I trying to achieve?" Chris explains. "Then, when I record, I can write down a scenario of what I see in the song and it's a great help to the players. They love it, because I don't have to explain the music. It gives the player an emotional feeling he can tune into."

'Into The Light' took three and a half months to complete, the longest time Chris had ever spent on one recording. He complained at the end of it, "Twelve hour days every day… when I did get time off, I would fly straight home to Dublin, only to have to turn round and come back to England almost as soon as I got there.

"I came off the road after 'Man On The Line', and took some time off for the first time in ages; I wanted to spend more time with Diane and Rosanna, and I wanted also to take some time off to begin getting the new album in shape. I was feeling very encouraged by the way things were developing around the world, and I wasn't particularly aiming in any real direction. The only thing I was certain about was that I wanted a far broader sound than I had on the past two records — so when Paul Hardiman came along, and we talked over what we could do, he just seemed so right. What I didn't realise was that Paul is not really a producer as such, he is more of an engineer (a function he performed on Kate Bush's 'Hounds Of Love' album), and the mantle of production fell on my shoulders more heavily than ever it had before. I always liked to be an onlooker, and just put my little bits in, but this time, I regard myself as the co-producer. I had a tremendous amount of input on this one, to the point that I've never worked so hard in my life." It reached the stage where Chris couldn't even control his own schedule — he spent Rosanna's second birthday sequestered in the studio, mixing 'Fire On The Water'.

The raw heart of the album was 'For Rosanna', written for his daughter, and — thankfully — a considerably less mawkish

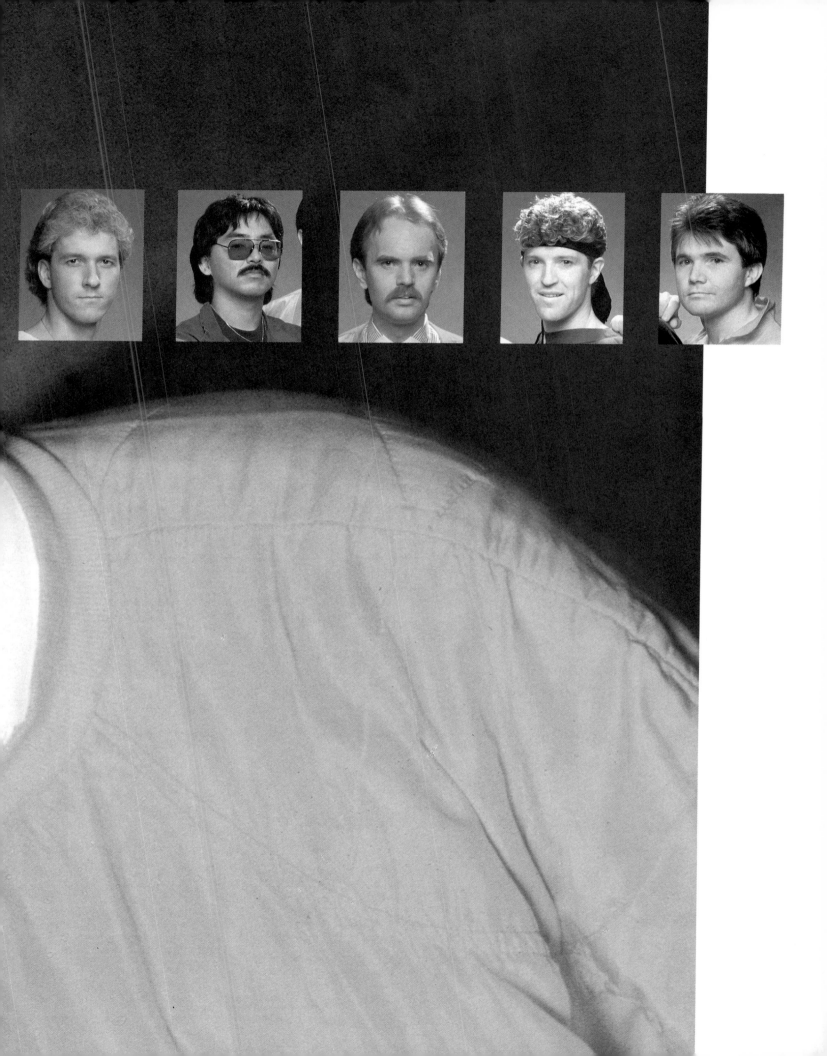

composition than such a description might suggest. A sparse duet for voice and piano, it was, says Chris, "A release and a therapy. When I recorded it I ran back into the studio to listen to it and I was in tears at the end because I'd actually managed to grab the emotion I was attempting to convey. It hit me right between the eyes. I also had a strong feeling that this was the best gift I'd ever given Rosanna. I know that in a quiet moment, when she's older and if she's had a row with her dad and her mother, she might just go away and listen to it. I'd like to think that any parent, having listened to the song, would identify with some of the thoughts and emotions that I had."

This is for Rosanna, sweet girl of mine
A song for the baby who changed my life
I'll never forget when I saw you first
I thought that my heart would burst
With the love that I have

Says Diane, "Rosanna takes it for granted that her dad does what he does. And she really isn't that impressed, it just seems normal to her. Chris has a video camera, which he is marvellous with; he's made all these tapes of her, and if Rosanna wants to just sit quietly, she'd much rather watch tapes of herself than see Chris on the telly — she's used to him now, whereas she isn't so accustomed to seeing herself on it."

'For Rosanna' was, quite unashamedly, a painful song to listen to, the sheer intensity of emotion touching nerves seldom affected by simple pop music. It also highlighted perhaps *the* reason why so much of Chris' music has come to receive such reverence as it does. He writes the truth, not the flowery poems and verbal convolutions which other writers might feel convey their meaning, confronting the listener head-on, with the barest minimum of subtlety. He says what people feel, but cannot express themselves, a remarkable gift which,

Right: On Killing Hill, near Dublin, 1984.

one might almost say thankfully, he uses but sparingly. Honesty, in this particular context, can be a harrowing experience.

It was with this in mind, perhaps, that elsewhere on the set, Chris turned his talents to more fanciful areas; the closing triumvirate of 'The Leader', 'The Vision' and 'What About Me' offered a blistering salvo of apocalyptic imagery inspired by a simple painting in a French hotel. "It depicted a group of warriors holding spears and wearing furs, standing in a semi-circle on a beach where the sea had gone out a long way. They were all looking up expectantly, waiting for something to happen, for their leader to return. And that's where the song began."

And I saw a burning chariot
And the four horsemen of the Apocalypse
Waiting on high
And I heard the thunder rolling in
And behold our leader on a pale horse riding in the sky

The similarities between this, and the Biblical Book of Revelations are deliberate:

And I looked, and behold a pale horse: and his name that sat on him was Death, and Hell followed with him.
(Revelations, 6:8)

'The Leader', *et al*, fit very snugly into Chris' growing canon of production epics, massive mood pieces targeted almost at giving the audience some kind of semi-mystical, vicarious thrill. Opening gently, the piece explodes with 'The Vision', a pyrotechnic display of provocative lyricism, before subsiding into the plaintive 'What About Me', the survivor of the holocaust *"left in the night, trembling with fear"*, and asking, *"Well, what about me?"*

Even as he recorded the song, Chris was well aware of the traps he was constructing for himself. "When you are making a statement on record, it isn't a matter of simply taking the front page of a newspaper and saying 'This is my statement', it's purely a part of a record. You're showing mental films. I am consistently being asked, as a 'Celebrity', to make remarks on different topics — social, political, whatever. Things that have nothing to do with the music. And it's stupid, they shouldn't be looking for celebrities, they should be looking for people who know what they're talking about. Just because I'm well known, it doesn't mean my opinion is more important than that of Joe Bloggs on the street — if anything, he's probably closer to it than I am. So when I sing of something of world-wide importance on a record, these things aren't meant to be taken seriously, commandments carved into stone, unless the listener particularly wants to. With 'The Leader', all I'm saying is 'If there's going to be

a nuclear war, there will be no winners.' It's nothing new (it was, in fact, a theme he had already broached on 'Transmission Ends', on 'Man On The Line'), I'm just presenting it in a way which I thought was different. The bottom line is, I have to write an album, and that song, and all the others which people pick out, for better or worse, as Supreme Statements, does not have a burning message for the world. It is simply part of the music."

Later, after the reviews of the British leg of the 'Into The Light' tour had been published, Chris returned to that particular theme, adding that while his fans were aware of exactly what he was attempting to put across, outsiders — and in the wake of 'The Lady In Red', there were a good number of those present — were often totally unprepared. "I couldn't believe some of the things that were

written. The critiques after the London shows were so vituperative that I realised I must have hit certain people on a really sore spot. Those guys sounded as if they'd all phoned each other up and asked what they ought to write. In some ways, I can sympathise with their point of view — when you come into something which is so big, and so popular, and you can't understand why, if you don't like it, then you make sure people know you don't like it. The only time it hurts me is when the fans are attacked, because it makes the fans feel stupid, either that or puts them so much on the defensive that in the end, they become as bigoted as the people who upset them in the first place. That's what I find offensive."

●   ●   ●

Shortly before Christmas, 1985, Chris appeared at the *Carol Aid* concert, a festive spoke within the *Band Aid* umbrella. The artists involved were those who appeared on the million-selling 'Now The Christmas Album' compilation, performing the songs included on that set; Chris' contribution, of course, was 'A Spaceman Came Travelling', presented on this occasion as a haunting solo performance. A week later he received an award for being the most successful songwriter ever to come out of Ireland, at an event designed to raise money for the Rehabilitation Institute.

Later, in May, Chris was a guest at the *Self Aid* show in Dublin, a charity event which included U2, Van Morrison and The Boomtown Rats. Chris' appearance was brief, almost impromptu, yet it probably earned a

because it brought home to people just how broad based Chris' support is."

The show was set up along the lines of the previous summer's *Live Aid* bash in London and Philadelphia, but this time its concerns were somewhat closer to home — Ireland's unemployment situation. "I must admit I was cynical about it," Chris later confessed. "I think unemployment is more than ever a government problem, and I think rock musicians are probably the worst people for preaching — they're usually so inarticulate. But then, I thought the worst thing that could happen was that the nation would be tuned into their own musical talents for 12 hours. Broadly, the show was not a success. But it was a good try."

Self Aid, then, was one of several charitable causes with which Chris has

Above: Maire Brennan, Bono, Bob Geldof and Chris at the Self Aid concert in Dublin. Opposite: Chris introducing the Duchess of York to the band at Wembley, 1986.

more honest response from the audience than any other that day. Again, he went onstage with just his guitar for support. "I felt that was all I needed. I knew that if I could get everybody singing loud enough to hear themselves, then I'd pull it off, they would do the rest. And they did."

Two months later, Kenny Thomson was still ecstatic as he relayed stories of a stadium full of fans singing, dancing and ghost guitaring their way through Chris' set. "They knew all the words, all the guitar solos, all the drum breaks. It was simply amazing, if only

involved himself, devotedly and — for the most part — silently. Only with the success, later in 1986, of 'Lady In Red', were his donations of money and gold discs to various children's charities publicised. The birth of Rosanna, against all odds as it seemed, had pointed him in that direction. In 1985 he was invited to appear at a charity function in aid of Birthright, an organisation involved in the fight against cot deaths, birth defects and infant mortality. "The event was at the Savoy Hotel, and there were about 250 people present, many of them top doctors, and there was an absolute rash of Royalty. Princess Diana is the patroness of the charity, and although she wasn't there, the Duke and Duchess of Gloucester, the Duchess of Westminster and the Duchess of Abercorn were. Everyone was most charming."

Chris was billed as the guest celebrity, and he played solo for 30 minutes — a short set, but one which survived a quiet start ("There was no booze, just natural food and drink") and developed quickly into a roaring success. "The Duchess of Gloucester came up and thanked me personally on several occasions," Chris said. "We raised about £14,000 — just amongst that many people."

Chris' charitable activities reached a peak in the summer of 1986 when he performed a 30 minute solo set at a Cork festival before 30,000 people, and his fee of more than £20,000 went directly to the Rotunda Hospital to buy much needed equipment for the maternity unit — three infant heart monitors and a cerebral function analysis monitor which can detect and avert possible brain damage and life-threatening situations in pre-term (premature) babies. "The knowledge that this equipment is working, and saving lives, has given me more lasting pleasure than anything else that happened to me in '86, including a UK number one!" says Chris.

As Chris predicted, 'Into The Light' was given a strong reception — and even when it did come in for a hard time from one of the papers, still Chris was able to celebrate, winning himself a case of wine when the writer in question conformed to Chris' expectations and used the same certain three adjectives ("One of which was 'Saccharine'") in his piece as Chris bet some friends he would. And although only *Melody Maker*, of all the British music papers, gave it more than a cursory mention in the news pages (they printed a brief review in the albums pages), the LP crashed into the UK Top 10 the week it was released, with advance orders which instantly qualified it for a gold disc.

"And short of coming in at number one, which is what it did throughout the rest of Europe, you really can't ask for anything more," Kenny Thomson says proudly. "The competition was incredible as well: Peter Gabriel's best record ever, new Queen, Madonna and Whitney Houston albums, Roxy Music and Cure compilations, a new Genesis album... he was in the best of company. And to be up there in the Top 10, meant he was already a very well established, very popular artist."

(At the time of going to press — March 1987 — UK sales of 'Into The Light' exceed 600,000 while Canadian sales exceed 300,000.)

The album entered the charts at the very top in Ireland, turning several shades of precious metal in the process. And it is the continued support of his adopted homeland which, perhaps, gives Chris more pleasure than that of all his other territories put together. Ireland was the first market to truly give its heart over to Chris, a distinction he has repaid by remaining there, and by remaining as visible as ever he was in the days before his career took off.

Far from closeting himself away in some dark mansion, he still steps out to go shopping or for a drink, and still smiles when he's stopped on the street by well-wishers. Only the packs of fans who occasionally drop by his home to stare, and the electronic gates which keep them from staring too much, separate his private life of today with that of 10 years ago. Kenny Thomson reckons Chris must have signed autographs for the entire population of Ireland simply from the number of times he's been cornered by admirers up against the dried fruit counter in the local supermarket!

Paul Tullio remembers one notable occasion when Chris, in the hope of going unrecognised for once, headed down to the shops in a raincoat with the collar up, and wearing a cap and glasses. Just as he was congratulating himself on finally pulling the wool over people's eyes, someone sidled up to him by the frozen foods counter, and said, simply, "Nice try with the hat, Chris." On another occasion, Chris decided it would be nice to go to the zoo for the day. "So, we kept calling him Dennis, in the hope that if people did recognise him, they wouldn't be too sure if it was him or just a lookalike, and wouldn't bother him. Of course, it didn't work... we were going round calling him Dennis in louder and louder voices, and he was still having to sign autographs!"

It is accepted, then, that Chris moves around the community; as Kenny Thomson says, "He has sustained his success in Ireland for more than 10 years, and to do that you have to be able to remove yourself from the star syndrome. Chris has done that very well. He very rarely hobnobs with other stars, largely because he has chosen to remain well outside of that circle. He's happier just staying in with his family, and maybe a few friends, nearly all of whom he has known since he was at University."

"Chris invited Mike and I to Rosanna's Christening," says Susan Colgan, "and the first thing we noticed was that we knew everybody there from way back. It's a lovely feeling, like being with family, and I think that has done an awful lot towards keeping Chris the way he is. To his fans, he is a great superstar, but when he's away from all that, he really is the same old Chris."

Even on the road, Chris retains the spirit which has always so endeared him to his friends. According to Kenny Thomson, "He has never gone in for riotous parties — it's a pretty strange thing. Because of the friendship

Above: Marseille, 1985.

in the band, the family atmosphere, our riotous parties are really stupid affairs, birthday parties with funny hats, that sort of thing. It's pretty tight — Chris much prefers being in a huddle with his band than he does getting involved in some wild rock 'n' roll abuse affair."

"He is very much into making home movies," says Susie Tullio. "Whenever he has people round for meals, he insists on filming them, usually hiding around corners and leaping out on them. But he's at his best when he's away on tour — he brings back films of the band, really crazy films with everybody trying to out-do everybody else. And there's usually Diane at the back, egging them all on."

And groupies? "Even in the early days," says Kenny without a trace of irony, "he was more likely to pick a girl up at the library than the stage door."

"I get girls knocking on the front door in the middle of the night," Chris told the *Sunday World*. "Phoning up at two in the morning to say, 'Hi, this is Louise, come on over to my place. It's a crazy scene.'" He declines politely. "Diane probably gets a little jealous, but she understands the scene well enough not to get upset about it. She believes it would be a different story if they had to wake up beside me in the morning, and put up with all my faults."

Chris' career in Britain finally exploded into the open in July, 1986. The first single from 'Into The Light', the dramatic 'Fire On The Water', stopped selling the moment the LP was released, and when A&M released the

UK follow-up, *New Musical Express* shrugged it off with the traditional prediction that nobody would buy it because they'd got the album already. But 'The Lady In Red' was made of stern stuff... and that despite both Chris and Kenny Thomson suggesting there were several far stronger candidates for single status on the LP. ('Fatal Hesitation', the much less successful follow-up to 'Lady In Red', was — in Chris' opinion at least — a far more viable prospect).

"We were under immediate pressure to release another single," says Chris, "and really the choice had already been made for us. When the album came out, particularly in Ireland, the song which everybody played was 'Lady In Red'. When I'd finished mixing that song, I remember, I said to Paul Hardiman, 'That's a number one. Wherever it is, wherever it's released, that is going to be a smash somewhere in the world.' And because it was being played so much, and would continue to be so whether we released it as a single or not, we really had no choice but to put it out. I didn't think it was the right time of year at all, though. I thought it would make a much better winter-time single. It wasn't a summer song at all!"

The version which made it onto the album was Chris' second attempt at recording the number. "We tried it first with the band, and it sounded horrible, it sounded like it could have been done in 1975. And it was a hard decision, but we threw the whole track out of the window and started again from scratch.

"What I tried to do was encapsulate a

moment," Chris said of the song. "It's about something which has happened to everybody in a relationship. You get used to your partner. Then one night you realise just how amazing they look, you're standing across the room and you think 'My God! Who is she?'"

The week before the single was released, Kenny Thomson spoke of his hopes for it. "I guarantee that with one Top 20 single, and the TV profile which would result, the floodgates would open. If we can sell a quarter of a million albums in Britain without a hit single, what would it be like if we did get one? It's quite frightening what Chris could achieve if he had a hit single."

Chris added, "I used to get embarrassed about having to point out I'd actually sold over a million albums in Britain, including three that went gold. The trouble is that the British public don't know you exist until you make the singles charts, appear on Top Of The Pops, and get picked upon by the papers. But the Top 10 arena doesn't really attract me because it relies too much on false images, passing trends and fashions. I've never really been all that interested in pursuing hit singles. The life of a single is so short, especially in this country. In France I had a number one which took eight months to climb all the way up the charts. But in Britain, the whole thing is over in five or six weeks."

'The Lady In Red' was written about Diane, but it struck a chord throughout the nation. Within a week of release, it had breached the British Top 40. Seven days later it stood at number 10. A fortnight after that, it was number one, outselling the previous chart topper, Madonna's 'Papa Don't Preach', by two to one, and helped on its way by the news that the Duke and Duchess of York, married the previous week, had taken a copy of the single on their honeymoon cruise.

"Romance is something most people get tongue-tied about," Chris explained. "It's great to have somebody else say it for you in a song." He revealed how one couple wrote and told him it had made their day to have the song played in church on their wedding day, and added: "It's meant a great deal to a lot of people. Many people must be able to see something of their own relationship in the song... even royalty!" And for the benefit of the daily papers, he even offered the Duke of York the opportunity to join him onstage. The offer wasn't accepted.

Chris celebrated the single's success quietly, with his wife, a bottle of champagne... and 14 press interviews in one day. Suddenly the 'Quiet Man of Pop' had become 'Chart-busting Chris de Burgh', the superstar whose "new anthem for the world's lovers... has made a million hearts swoon." The London *Daily Mirror* devoted an entire centre spread to Chris and Diane, a banner headline "Here she is! The Lady In Red"

subtitled "We reveal the woman the whole country is talking about", and followed it up with a competition — "Meet Chris de Burgh and win a super television!" It was hard to say which prize they rated highest!

"It was astonishing to see, first hand, how the spotlight — when it hits you — is just white, totally blinding. I just went along with it, although some of the things which I said, in good faith, were so completely distorted. One paper asked me how I celebrated the hit, so I told them; we'd just moved house, the place was still in uproar, but we had friends coming over in the evenings to celebrate the single, celebrate the new house, and so on. And it came out in the paper that I'd been out every night drinking champagne and Guinness... The difference between what I said, and what was printed, was so vast. All in all, it was quite incredible."

Compliant though he was, Chris drew the line at having his family roped into the circus, to the extent of refusing even to allow press photographers to fly over to take family snapshots. "Every newspaper, every Sunday magazine, wanted to fly photographers to Ireland to take family pictures, which I refused to let them do. Instead, I got Diane's brother to do one session, of three family shots, to distribute to the papers, so I felt I held on to some credibility." Even if the price was the bad press which is the Fourth Estate's last resort when it finds itself thwarted. "In Germany, one magazine asked if I would pose for some pictures with Diane for them. I'd already drawn the line about that in England; besides, Diane had gone shopping, so we couldn't have done it even if we'd wanted to. The German press do seem to want to know an awful lot about your private life, and in this instance, the guy went away and wrote a story about my being 'insanely jealous' and 'keeping my wife in the background'."

Diane, at least, was grateful for this. While the single was in the charts, she was to become almost as great a media personality as Chris himself, and she admits, "It did get a little embarrassing, although, having just moved house, I was so busy with the house that I wasn't really aware of it. It's only later, when I look back, that I realise the whole of that summer is a complete blur. Chris was forever having to fly in and out of London for interviews and television appearances, so at the time, we were so grateful just to have some time together that we didn't even mention what was going on. The only time I was actually confronted by it was when I went shopping in the local village, and all the local kids would sing the song as I went by.

"But people shouldn't bother about what I think or do. It's Chris' career, he does all the work. In fact, the Chris I know is nothing like the Chris his fans know. Some people dissect his songs, analyse them, read things into them

which simply aren't intended, and they come out of it viewing him as some very serious, God-like figure who can do no wrong. And he isn't. If he was, I'd have to wake up in the morning, every morning, and squeal 'Ooh, it's CHRIS DE BURGH!', then rush to fix his breakfast. I don't do that, and he wouldn't want me to. He's very serious about his career, but away from that, he really is just a normal person. He plays jokes on his friends, his friends do it back to him, they abuse him, they laugh at him, and laugh with him.

"A lot of it has to do with the fact that, living in Dublin, we are so insulated. He isn't continually being built up by other 'Rock Stars'; most of our friends are professional people, doctors, lawyers, that kind of thing, and in a way, I think he sees the work they do as being far more important than anything he could ever do."

"Very often, Chris will be up to something or other, and we say to him, 'If only your fans could see you now'," says Susie Tullio. "One afternoon we all went out to a tea room in Wicklow, this lovely quiet place with old ladies nodding off at the other tables. Suddenly, Chris decided to pile all the cups and saucers on top of one another, and try to fill them all with tea. Of course, there was tea cascading everywhere, all over the table, all over the floor... which is when the waitress came out. She simply couldn't believe what was happening, Chris de Burgh, her hero, pouring tea all over the floor!"

•   •   •

The media hysteria (Burghiemania?) continued, unabated, when the Duke and Duchess of York attended the first of Chris' shows at London's Wembley Arena. Or, as *The Sun* newspaper put it, "The Royal newly-weds will bop to their favourite Lady In Red star, Chris de Burgh... The former number one became the theme for the sweethearts' honeymoon after Andy said it reminded him of Fergie's flaming red hair." And the morning after the show, Fleet Street sub-editors had a field day as they accompanied the evening's photos of Chris, Diane and the Duchess — herself clad in red — with such headlines as "Ladies In Red", "The Lady In Red", "My Lady In Red"... "Royalty never brings out the best in headline writers," Chris joked later.

By mid-June, Chris and the band had undertaken 120 gigs, to more than one million people, a phenomenally successful outing which saw him returning again and again to countries which didn't see enough of him the first time around. Before Christmas, for instance, Chris played 32 shows in Germany alone, but by February he was back again, this time for a dozen nights which included three at the Dortmund Hall, the biggest venue in the country holding 18,500 people. Needless to say, every single show sold out. And it wasn't

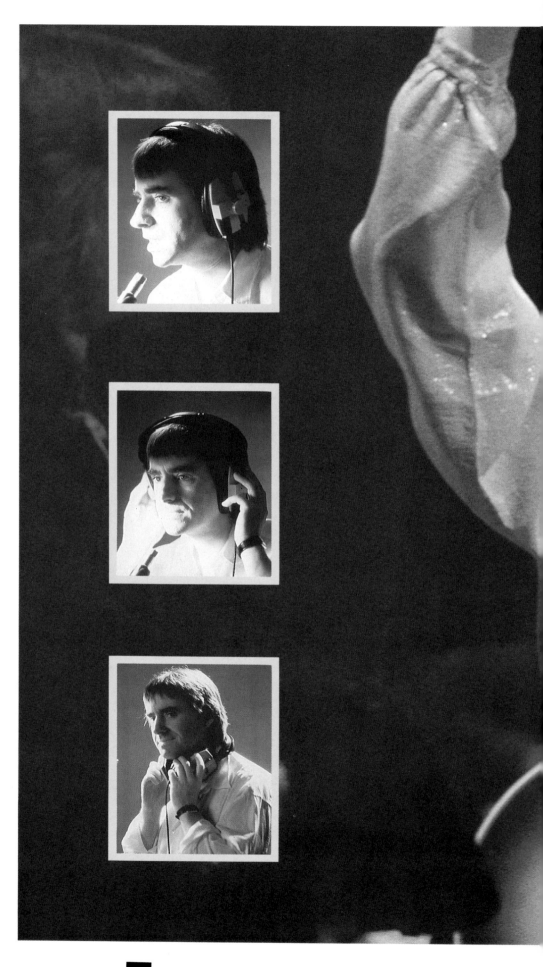

only in Germany that the 'Into the Light' tour left attendance records in shreds. Twelve performances in Dublin (of which 8 were consecutive) *trebled* that particular auditorium's best. Over 150,000 ticket applications were received for the shows.

The tour also took Chris to Spain for the first time as a performer — he had previously seen the country only as a tourist — while Australia gave him one of the most rousing receptions he had ever received anywhere. 'Lady In Red' had hit the number two spot there, the album had gone platinum, but as Chris himself says, the locals still didn't really know what to expect ..."and neither did we! But they couldn't have made me feel more welcome."

From Australia, the tour made its way to Los Angeles, en route for the Canadian shows, 'Lady In Red' was just breaking into the American chart (it eventually peaked at number 3) and the same week became the number One selling single on the Billboard Sales Chart and while Chris believes "You would have to be crazy to tour the States on the back of a ballad," he was more than happy to make a brief stop over to appear on the Joan Rivers Show. Later, he was invited on to Johnny Carson's show as well, but had to decline "because I was in Newfoundland, on the Canadian tour, at the time."

'Into The Light' followed the single into the U.S. Top 20 chart, of course, earning a gold disc in the process, and elsewhere around the world, similar awards simply piled up. Gold discs were awarded in Israel, New Zealand, Sweden, Denmark and Belgium; in Norway, South Africa and Greece platinum discs were called for, in Switzerland and England double platinum; in Ireland and Canada, *triple* platinum, "And the single was even bigger than the album," Chris says, proudly revealing that it had topped the chart in *fourteen* countries, including "some which I didn't even know had a chart — Singapore and the Philippines, for instance". In fact, by summer, 1987, 'The Lady In Red' had made the Top 5 in every country where it was released, with Chris planning to record a Spanish language version of the song in order to take the conquests even further afield.

In February, also, Chris was nominated for two of the awards at the annual British Phonographic Institute ceremony, a beanfeast designed to honour the 'Best' in British pop of the previous year. A hot favourite to scoop at least one of the categories — Best Male Artist and Best Single — Chris eventually left the Grosvenor Hotel empty-handed, pipped in the first instance by Peter Gabriel, in the second by the somewhat more fleeting attractions of the Pet Shop Boys. George Martin and Adam Faith were just two of the people present who afterwards expressed some amazement at the latter. Chris, however, had no time for recriminations or regrets; he had a tour to complete.

The first leg of the 'Into The Light' tour had been scheduled — and sold out — long before the album kicked a whole new army of potential ticket-buyers into action. Shows which, prior to the success of 'Lady In Red', had already been well over-subscribed, were suddenly flung into such a state of siege that there was now no alternative but to tack further dates on to the itinerary — in many countries, demand was so high that a second tour, throughout February 1987, was scheduled, taking Chris not only back to venues he had packed out but four months previous, but also to a handful of others omitted from the original schedule. The first shows had been Chris' acknowledgement of his long time fans; the new ones were his Thank You to the more recent arrivals.

"Every time we tour, it seems audiences go further across the board," he said. "The majority of the fans at the concert tend to be the 15-25 year olds, but it's not unusual to see middle-aged couple going crazy along with everybody else. At one show there were three people, a grandmother, a mother and a teenager, sitting together with a banner saying 'Thank you from three generations of Chris de Burgh fans'. And it's the same everywhere we play, in Germany, Canada, Ireland, Scandinavia, France, Britain, everywhere, which is great. Because it shows I am not limited to just one group of people. My music cuts across age barriers and musical barriers, and it is my ability to do that which I value above all others, because that is how I started, putting on a show simply to entertain the guests at the hotel, and trying to make them all feel involved in the music. And that is what I am still trying to do today. I'm not interested in making it as a Rock musician, a Folk musician, or anything else; I just want to make it as a Musician. A Musician and an Entertainer. And as long as I can do that, I'm happy."

In October, 1986, the magazine *Record Collector* ran a fairly lengthy examination of Chris' recorded career, highlighting the fact that, since the success of 'The Lady In Red', the value to collectors of his back catalogue had changed literally over-night from being of minority interest only, to very big business indeed, particularly in the United Kingdom; else-where, Chris' career was already so well established that a thriving market in his earliest, long-deleted, releases had long before been recognised. Even there, however, interest in his back catalogue exploded. When 'Eastern Wind' hit number one in Norway, all four of its predecessors swiftly followed it onto the listings, whilst in other lands, where his name was not so well known that the release of every new album precipi-tated a mad rush on local record stores, any one of his albums was as likely to enjoy an upsurge of popularity at any given moment, simply as a result of people finally deciding to buy a record by that guy they'd heard on the radio so often.

While the majority of Chris' albums have always been available in one form or another, his singles usually enjoyed but a very brief lifespan, particularly in the days before 'Don't Pay The Ferryman'. The interest awakened in his career by 'Into The Light' and 'The Lady In Red', saw a quite unprece-dented demand for Chris' earliest singles, most of which had previously been readily available to those collectors willing to expend the necessary time and energy in seeking them out, but which were now acquiring price tags which threatened to place Chris amongst the most collectable artists of the mid-1980s.

The following discography is of UK releases only; how-ever, the releases world-wide have been remarkably consistent, with only a handful of alternate couplings finding their way onto the shelves. Elsewhere, catalogue numbers, and pack-aging alone differ. In this context, one thinks immediately of the French single which coupled 'Sailor' with 'Wall Of Silence' (AMS 7696) around the time of the 'Eastern Wind' album, and more recently, the Spanish 'Lady In Red', backed by 'Borderline'. There are also several interesting Dutch pairings; 'Record Company Bash' as the flip of 'The Traveller', 'Don't Pay The Ferryman' backed with 'Living On An Island', and an EP which brings together 'A Spaceman Came Travelling', 'Where Peaceful Waters Flow', 'The Head And The Heart' and 'Perfect Day' (A&M 3900707).

'A Spaceman Came Travelling' has, to date, made appearances in *eight* different guises, worldwide. In its original form, on the 'Spanish Train' album, it lasted five minutes and 10 seconds; as a single the following year, cuts from the intro and the outro reduced it to four minutes, five seconds, while 1984 saw a version released (on the flip of the 'Borderline' single) which was just three minutes and 30 seconds! A similar edit appeared on the Dutch 'Moonlight And Vodka' single, although in the remastering of the song, the actual perfor-mance was slowed down sufficiently for the song to clock in at four minutes and five seconds. The aforementioned Dutch EP edit, with four seconds cut from the coda followed, as did a hitherto unreleased in-concert rendering (on the U.K. 'I Love The Night' 12" single). Finally, pressure from Chris' UK record company led to the song appearing once more, in time for Christmas 1986, in a substantially remixed form with a new vocal performance. "I thought the original had been out enough," Chris smiled. "I wanted to give people something different."

This was also the logic behind the live version of the song released in 1984, on the first of Chris' 12" singles. The day has long since passed when 12" releases were considered somehow collectable — today, even the most 'limited' edition is still pressed in quantities which defy anybody to believe themselves to have purchased a future rarity, and their value to collectors is gauged instead by the amount of elsewhere unavailable material contained therein. This particular rendering of 'A Spaceman' aside, however, Chris' 12" singles to date have been particularly unadventurous, sharing with their 7" contem-poraries, a tendency merely to plug the LP catalogue. The remix of the 'Don't Pay The Ferryman' single, which was released shortly before 'The Getaway' album aside, Chris' 45 RPM catalogue has been startlingly unadventurous, which makes its current popularity seem all the more surprising (1981's 'Waiting For The Hurricane'/'Broken Wings' live ver-sion pairing might have still proved tempting to those fans of Chris who don't want to pay out for the rest of the 'Best Moves' album, although there doesn't seem to be too many of them!).

Perhaps because of this, Chris' Promotional singles have thus far been ignored by all but the most fanatical collectors; the sole exception being that which coupled 'High On Emotion' with 'Much More Than This'. The latter was never officially made available on single, and appears here primarily as a sop to English disc jockey Jonathan King. A long time admirer of Chris, he played the song incessantly on his radio programme, each week imploring his listeners to harrass A&M into releasing it on 45. Weekly, too, the *No Limits* television show, which Jonathan produced, featured the song as a chart contender, again without any indication that it was to be given full single status; finally, out of sheer frustration, he gave out the home phone number of the head of A&M, and instructed his listeners to make the poor man's life a misery until he bowed to their demands. And in 1987, with 'Much More Than This' *still* far from the release schedules, he was still singing its praises, cornering Chris at the B.P.I. Awards cere-mony in London to tell him the song still had what it took to top the chart...

In terms of albums, only one stands out as an obvious collectable. 'Far Beyond These Castle Walls', Chris' first album, has appeared in three formats, at least in the U.K.; the 1975 original, a 1982 mid-price reissue, and finally a budget priced repackaging replete with a new, and vastly inferior, sleeve. Of these, the two A&M sets have both appreciated in value over the years.

One final area remains of interest to the collector, the compact disc market, now overcoming the teething problems which were originally posed by the high prices attached to both discs and equipment; as yet, Chris' catalogue offers nothing which has been omitted from the regular vinyl discs, but as record companies strive to make the infant prodigy seem even more desirable, it can only be a matter of time before *something* appears which will send the Completeists hurrying out to invest in the format.

albums

31.1.75
FAR BEYOND THESE CASTLE WALLS
(A&M AMLH 68284)
Hold On/The Key/Windy Night/Sin City/New Moon/ Watching The World/ Lonesome Cowboy/Satin Green Shutters/Turning Round/ Goodnight

7.11.75
SPANISH TRAIN & OTHER STORIES
(A&M AMLH 68343)
Spanish Train/Lonely Sky/This Song For You/Patricia The Stripper/A Spaceman Came Travelling/I'm Going Home/ The Painter/Old Friend/The Tower/Just Another Poor Boy

5.8.77
AT THE END OF A PERFECT DAY
(A&M AMLH 64647)
Broken Wings/Round And Around/I Will/Summer Rain/ Discovery/Brazil/In A Country Churchyard/A Rainy Night In Paris/If You Really Love Her, Let Her Go/Perfect Day

26.1.79
CRUSADER
(A&M AMLH 64746)
Carry On/I Had The Love In My Eyes/Something Else Again/The Girl With April In Her Eyes/Just In Time/The Devil's Eye/It's Such A Long Way Home/Old Fashioned People/Quiet Moments/ Crusader/You And Me

4.7.80
EASTERN WIND
(A&M AMLH 64815)
The Traveller/The Record Company Bash/Tonight/Wall of Silence/Flying Home/ Shadows And Lights/Some Things Never Change/Tourist Attraction/Eastern Wind

28.8.81
BEST MOVES
(A&M AMLH 68532)
The Traveller/Every Drop Of Rain/In A Country Churchyard/Patricia The Stripper/Satin Green Shutters/ Spanish Train/Waiting For The Hurricane/Broken Wings (live)/Lonely Sky/Spaceman Came Travelling/Crusader

3.82
FAR BEYOND THESE CASTLE WALLS (reissue)
(A&M AMID 119)

1.10.82
THE GETAWAY
(A&M AMLH 68549)
Don't Pay The Ferryman/ Living On The Island/Crying & Laughing/I'm Counting On You/The Getaway/Ship To Shore/All The Love I Have Inside/Borderline/Where Peaceful Waters Flow/The Revolution/Light A Fire/ Liberty

7.5.84
MAN ON THE LINE
(A&M AMLX 65002)
The Ecstasy Of Flight/Sight And Touch/Taking It To The Top/The Head And The Heart/ The Sound Of A Gun/High On Emotion/Much More Than This/Man On The Line/ Moonlight And Vodka/ Transmission Ends

1984
FAR BEYOND THESE CASTLE WALLS (second reissue) *(Pickwick SHM 3151)*

3.12.84
THE VERY BEST OF CHRIS DE BURGH *(Telstar SPAR 2248)*
Don't Pay The Ferryman/The Ecstasy Of Flight/The Traveller/Ship To Shore/Flying Home/Satin Green Shutters/ A Spaceman Came Travelling/ Spanish Train/High On Emotion/Borderline/Lonely Sky/In A Country Churchyard/ Patricia The Stripper/Waiting For The Hurricane

22.5.86
INTO THE LIGHT
(A&M AMA 5121)
Last Night/Fire On The Water/The Ballroom Of Romance/The Lady In Red/Say Goodbye To It All/The Spirit Of Man/Fatal Hesitation/One Word/For Rosanna/The Leader/The Vision/What About Me

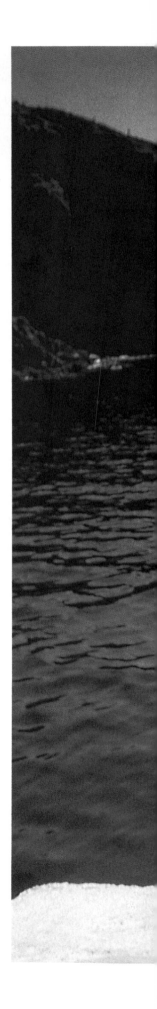

singles (UK releases only)

14.2.75
Hold On/Sin City
(A&M AMS 7148)

11.7.75
Flying/Watching The World
(A&M AMS 7182)

30.1.76
Lonely Sky/This Song For You
(A&M AMS 7196)

23.4.76
Patricia the Stripper/Old
Friend (A&M AMS 7224)

11.76
A Spaceman Came Travelling/
Just Another Poor Boy
(A&M AMS 7267)

5.8.77
Summer Rain/Rainy Night In
Paris (A&M AMS 7305)

14.10.77
Broken Wings/I Will
(A&M AMS 7320)

27.1.78
Discovery/Round And Round
(A&M AMS 7336)

10.3.78
Spanish Train/Perfect Day
(A&M AMS 7347)

2.2.79
I Had The Love In My Eyes/
Just In Time
(A&M AMS 7416)

30.3.79
The Devil's Eye/Long Way
Out (A&M AMS 7430)

25.7.80
Shadows & Lights/Walls Of
Silence (A&M AMS 7545)

3.10.80
The Traveller/Eastern Wind
(A&M AMS 7562)

28.8.81
Waiting For The Hurricane/
Broken Wings (live)
(A&M AMS 8160)

6.11.81
A Spaceman Came Travelling/
Patricia The Stripper
(A&M AMS 8182)

17.9.82
Don't Pay The Ferryman/All
The Love I Have Inside
(A&M AMS 8256)

26.11.82
The Getaway/Living On The
Island (A&M AMS 8268)

11.2.83
Ship To Shore/Crying And
Laughing (A&M AMS 8309)

30.4.84
High On Emotion/The Vision
(A&M AM 190)

23.7.84
I Love The Night/Moonlight
And Vodka (A&M AM 202)

23.7.84
I Love The Night/Moonlight &
Vodka/Don't Pay The
Ferryman/A Spaceman Came
Travelling (live)
(A&M AMX 202)

3.12.84
A Spaceman Came Travelling/
Borderline (A&M AM 225)

11.2.85
Sight And Touch/Taking It To
The Top (A&M AM 237)

20.3.86
Fire On The Water/The Vision
(A&M AM 317)

20.3.86
Fire On The Water/The
Vision/The Leader/What
About Me (A&M AMY 317)

27.6.86
The Lady In Red/Say Goodbye
To It All (A&M AM 331)

27.6.86
The Lady In Red/Say Goodbye
To It All/Don't Pay The
Ferryman (A&M AMY 331)

5.9.86
Fatal Hesitation/The Ecstasy
Of Flight (I Love The Night)
(A&M AM 346)

28.11.86
A Spaceman Came Travelling/
The Ballroom Of Romance
(A&M AM 365)

28.11.86
A Spaceman Came Travelling/
The Ballroom Of Romance
(A&M AMX 365)

ACKNOWLEDGEMENTS:

For all their help during the writing of this book, I would like to extend my grateful thanks to Chris Allen, Chris Charlesworth, Mike and Susan Colgan, Diane Davison, Dennis at Bury St.Edmunds, Doug Flett, Derek Green, Jo-Ann Greene, Ian Kojima, Ned Ludd, Dave Margereson, Al Marnie, Danny McBride, James Morris, Glen Morrow, Jeff Phillips, Charlie Prevost, Kenny Thomson, Paul and Susie Tullio, everybody at Mismanagement and the New C de B Fan Club, and finally, to Chris himself.

DAVE THOMPSON, *June 1987.*